Hugh Leonard was born in Dublin in 1926 and was educated at Presentation College, Dun Laoghaire. He then spent fourteen years as a clerk in the Land Commission until he began to have some success as a playwright. He was Literary Editor of the Abbey Theatre from 1976 until 1977 and is a member of the council of the Dublin Theatre Festival. His other plays include *A Leap in the Dark* (1957), *A Walk on the Water* (1960), *The Saints Go Cycling In* (1965), *The Au Pair Man* (1968), *The Patrick Pearse Motel* (1971), *Thieves* (1973), *Summer* (1974), *Irishmen* (1975), *Time Was* (1976), *Moving Days* (1981), *Kill* (1982), *Scorpions* (1983) and *The Mask of Moriarty* (1985). His real breakthrough came with *Da*, which in the United States won a Tony Award for the Best Play of 1978, the Drama Desk Award and the New York Critics' Circle Award. He also won the Harvey Award for the best play of 1979/80 with *A Life*. His latest play, *Moving*, was produced at the Abbey Theatre in 1992.

Hugh Leonard has written a number of plays for television, including *Silent Song*, which won the Italia Award for 1967, and his adaptations for television include works by Emily Brontë, Dickens, Flaubert, Maugham and Saki. His four-part drama series, *Parnell and the Englishwoman*, was shown on BBC Television in 1991, and his novel of the same name is published by Penguin. Penguin also publishes *Home before Night*, his autobiography, and its companion volume, *Out after Dark* Hugh Leonard lives in Dalkey, outside Dublin, and writes a weekly satirical column for the *Sunday Independent* in between what he calls 'real work'.

HUGH LEONARD

ROVER AND OTHER CATS

ILLUSTRATED BY WILLIAM GELDART

PENGUIN BOOKS

PENGUIN BOOKS

Published by the Penguin Group
Penguin Books Ltd, 27 Wrights Lane, London W8 5TZ, England
Penguin Books USA Inc., 375 Hudson Street, New York, New York 10014, USA
Penguin Books Australia Ltd, Ringwood, Victoria, Australia
Penguin Books Canada Ltd, 10 Alcorn Avenue, Toronto, Ontario, Canada M4V 3B2
Penguin Books (NZ) Ltd, 182–190 Wairau Road, Auckland 10, New Zealand

Penguin Books Ltd, Registered Offices: Harmondsworth, Middlesex, England

First published by André Deutsch Ltd 1992
Published in Penguin Books 1993
1 3 5 7 9 10 8 6 4 2

Printed in England by Clays Ltd, St Ives plc

Contents

For Julia Carty
– these many cats, to help make up
for the last one

Overture

THEY COME silently by moonlight, the cats.

You can hear their shadows brush across the patch of balding grass that separates our apartment from where the granite rocks elbow one another into the sea. One by one, the cats make themselves comfortable, sitting in the charmed circles of their tails that are like ribbons on Christmas packages. They look up at my workroom window, this quarter century of cats.

There is the trio of Honey, Priscilla and Tinkle; then come Oscar, Rover, Dubh and even Gatsby, who was never mine and yet is. Behind them, lost in the dark along the foreshore, is James Joyce's Martello tower at Sandycove; further away are the lights along the East

Pier at Dun Laoghaire and the yellow face of the town hall clock. Beyond, like pinpoints, are the lights of Dublin tracing the line of the bay and toiling up the hill of Howth.

Six of the seven cats have come in protest. They want to know why Rover's name and not one of theirs is in the title of my book. As for Rover himself, he has been summonsed to present the case for the defence, but it is a balmy summer night and he has already dozed off. He could never in any case concentrate for long; twice, I swear, I saw him trip while going upstairs and once he fell off the kitchen table and could not be bothered to land on his feet.

I explain to the plaintiffs that Rover is an uncommon name for a cat and that a book needs a catchy title. At this, Honey wrinkles her elegant Siamese nose in disdain. Rover, she says, achieved nothing in his entire life unless one counts the November evening when the Dun Laoghaire fire brigade and half the police force of South County Dublin came to his rescue, and to this day they speak of him in fire station and barracks as the Cat that Never Was. 'Thanks to Mr Rover,' Honey tells me, 'you and herself inside are known as the "quare ones". Whereas I' – and she sniffs as if it was two sardines to talk to her – 'was the inspiration for the Perfect Crime.'

There is a purring of general agreement at this.

It is now Tinkle's turn to miaow. He, like Rover, is a ginger tom and argues that there is nothing to choose between the pair of them. 'After all,' he argues, 'what's in a name?'

'Phrase-maker!' Oscar growls at him. Oscar is black and white and proof positive that a cat can scowl. He is the spitting (and hissing and snarling) image of Sylvester in the cartoon films – the one that the canary, Tweetie Pie, called a puddy tat.

Priscilla says nothing, perhaps because of an acute personal problem, and it is that in spite of a name as feminine as crinolines or the colour pink, he is in fact a he. And when a chap is addressed as Prissie for short, he thinks twice before putting in his interference.

As for Gatsby, being a blow-in, he has really no argument at all. His home – he is the only one of the seven who is not yet a ghost – is a full two miles away in Glenageary and he has never even set paw inside our apartment. He is a red-point Siamese and sits, a solitary bookend. I ask him why he has come. He sniffs, crosses his eyes, says 'Because' and pretends to be inscrutable.

That leaves Dubh (his name is the Irish for 'black'). The one small patch of white glows on his chest in the dark, and I know that with his paws he is making bread on the inch-high grass. He fixes his amber eyes on me and gives a soft 'Wah', which was his cry and his song.

He is saying that I loved him best, and wants to know why on that account this is not his book. I tell him that if it were, I should never finish it for tears. The yellow lights blink slowly in benison.

I had better make a start . . . .

Honey

PAULE FOUND Honey's pedigree form the other day. She was a Scorpio, and a Scots lass, born in Coupar Angus, Perthshire, on November 7th, 1965. Two months later, I bought her for twelve guineas at the Regent Pet Stores in Camden Town. A bag of cat litter and a book on the care of Siamese cats cost another nine-and-sixpence. Even for those days, happiness came cheap at £13 1s 6d.

We lived in an apartment block in SW13, where, whenever a north wind blew down Castelnau and across Barnes Common, my wife's two handbags turned green from mildew. The flat was base camp in our assault on London; already the deposit had been paid on a house in Barnes itself, with a rose garden and a back gate that opened on to the very grass of the village green. For eight months in every year, I wrote scripts for television; the other four were set aside for a stage play.

We gave not much thought to the future. Once, at a TV awards dinner, I asked, more from idleness than real concern: 'What happens to old television writers?' My answer was a blank stare that went around the table like a decanter of port. Ours was a trade as yet too new for anyone to have grown old in. For myself, I was thirty-seven, with a wife and an eight-year-old daughter who had been promised a Siamese kitten.

Friday, January 7th, Camden Town, rush hour. I nudged the Rover into a one-way system. The kitten, paid for and on my daughter's lap, miaowed feebly.

'Dad, I think it's sick.'

'Nonsense.' (I wondered if it would live until we reached the flat.) 'Now hold it, but don't maul it.'

'I'm not.'

'Danielle, will you control it? It'll crawl under the brake pedal.'

'Dad . . .'

'What?'

'Dad, it's doing *pipi*' (my wife is Belgian, and it rubs off).

'Let it.'

'In my hand, Dad.'

'Lower the window – not too far – and shake your hand dry.'

A car behind us hooted when we failed to make the signalled left turn.

At home, we pored over the pedigree form. The seal-point's parents were Kirone and Geno Janetto, and one of her great-grandmothers was Honey Bee, and so Danielle, whom we call Dan because the hoped-for diminutive of 'Dany' never caught on, named her Honey. Once christened, the kitten rolled around for a bit and came to rest face upwards, and, mistaking languor for coquettishness, I committed the *lèse majesté* of prodding her with a forefinger. The immediate reaction was a kind of multiple acupuncture. Four paws, each equipped, I think, with a dozen needles, closed upon and into the finger. Then, as if to show that nothing but the best was good enough for the kind of person she now owned, Honey went to work with her teeth as well. Introductions were complete.

Three months later, we moved into the house on the village green. When the removals men had gone and Honey came out of hiding, I put on my English squire's face and strolled the hundred or so yards to the Sun Inn. I detest thin ale very nearly as much as the thin glasses it is served up in, but the occasion had to be risen to. I owned my first house, all red brick and

stockbroker tudor, and had a wife, a daughter and a
Siamese. As it transpired, that was also the day on
which I had my first glimpse of Priscilla.

On the way back from the Sun, such sheer happiness
overcame me that I gave an almighty kick to a twig
that was lying on the path. I then watched as, closely
pursued by my right shoe, it described a graceful para-
bola and fell, not to earth, but into the village pond.

The shoe did not sink; rather, it floated with the kind
of insouciance of a small boat that had been to Dunkirk
and back. Two or three people stopped to look, their
eyes segueing from my stockinged foot to the bobbing
shoe. They waited in silence. Back home in Dublin, and
if this were a pond in Stephen's Green or Herbert Park,
I would have been addressed reverently and with senti-
ments of comfort: e.g. 'Jazus, weren't you the lucky
whoor that your leg didn't go with it?' The present
onlookers, however, were British and had the seemly
reticence of their race.

There was nothing for it but to remove the other shoe
and both socks, roll up my trouser legs and wade out,
praying that the pond contained no broken bottles. The
water was knee deep and April-cold. A few uncertain
steps brought the shoe almost within reach; then I
heard a sudden hissing noise. My heart withered as
from the little island in the centre of the pond a stately
swan emerged and bore down on the trespasser. I had

an insane memory of Laurel and Hardy in *Swiss Miss* trying to carry an upright piano along a swaying rope bridge and meeting a gorilla at the half-way point. As the gap narrowed, the wings began to unfurl and the hissing became angrier. I addressed the swan, out loud and damn the spectators, who by now had swollen in number and were standing at the water's edge as if to watch a returning round-the-world yachtsman capsize at the harbour mouth. This was no time for pride. I explained to the bird that the shoe was the extent of my territorial demands. An isolated offence. Willing to enter into a bond. Mercy of the court. Five pounds in the poor box.

The plea worked. The swan applied reverse throttle in a swirl of pond-water, glared, hissed out a conditional discharge, came about and set course for home, a dreadnought disdaining to fire upon a puffer.

When I regained dry land, the onlookers flitted off like bats in twilight. One of them forgot himself insofar as to murmur 'Well done, sir,' then he, too, was gone. And yet, standing bare-footed, I was not alone. The handsomest cat I had ever seen had been watching my adventure from a nearby gatepost. It was small of head, long-haired and could have been a Persian; its tail was a plume of such magnificence that it almost wore the cat. Even shivering and with damp clay underfoot, I said: 'Hello, puss.' He – it was Priscilla – turned himself into a shadow; tall grass swallowed him.

Later on, it occurred to me that I had been auditioned as a future provider. Prissy, as he was informally known, lived with a gentle, elderly lady named Miss King. It is a hard world for cats, and they know it. Their owners – I write the word with mirthless laughter – sometimes fall ill and die, so an understudy becomes one of life's necessities. A man who could lose a shoe in a village pond, wade in after it and talk to a swan was easy meat. No, not meat; he was tuna-fish and pilchards. A cat must live.

Months passed. Prissy's hour had not yet come, but I caught glimpses of him as he sailed over back garden fences in a kind of balletic steeplechase. Meanwhile, Honey went from kitten to petite cat. With Siamese coquetry, she pretended not to enjoy company, and yet always placed herself downstage-centre whenever we had house guests. These were usually Irish actors who, since they were in a TV play of mine, felt that the least Paule and I could do was provide board and lodging as compensation for depriving them of their loved ones back in Donnybrook or Clontarf.

Most of our Irish friends liked to drink to excess, on the principle that otherwise they might as well not drink at all. I was more at ease with these than with our one or two abstainer friends, who were members of the Pioneer movement and wore the small lapel badge depicting the Sacred Heart performing auto-surgery. One knows where one is with a drunk, but teetotalism in an Irishman is unnatural; if it is not checked, he becomes unpredictable and repays watching. One of our non-drinking actor guests was a case in point. During his stay with us, he regularly received letters from both his wife and his woman friend. We always knew when the latter had written, for no sooner had the post come than he would seize an orange from a bowl in the kitchen and bear it and the letter upstairs to the lavatory. There, behind a bolted door, he would let his passion run riot by forcing the orange, unpeeled, around the U-bend.

He was a native of Cork, which has a strong puritanical tradition, and the ritual with the oranges may have been a substitute for a love that dared not speak its name. At any rate, his secret vice came to light a few days after his departure when a plumber, investigating a blockage, cut through an outside pipe and was almost brained by an avalanche of Jaffas. (Admittedly, the letters that provoked this minor fetish could have been written by his wife rather than his inamorata, but one likes to take the romantic view.)

Another of our house guests was a prodigious drinker until he and the stuff gave each other up, whereupon he fell in love with an Irishwoman named Hastings. Being happily married, the mother of two and a devout mass-goer, she put a flea in his ear, and, without vodka-and-bitter-lemon for solace, he fell into an abyss of moping. One morning, he left our house for what were then the ABC studios at Teddington Lock, but in his distraught condition boarded the wrong train. While the television company frantically sent out search parties, he was sitting on the station platform at St Margaret's under a huge British Rail hoarding which said: 'Why Don't You Go to Hastings?'

By contrast, our drinking friends behaved as impeccably as their verticality allowed. Our Honey had a soft spot for tipplers, and would often sit at the head of the stairs, to await a homecoming that on a good night was rich in incident. We had bought our house from the principal of a school of art, a much-loved man whose star pupils, to mark his retirement, had embellished the stairwell with a vast mural. The stairs were in three short flights, one at right angles to the next, and the finished landscape resembled the kind of wall painting one would see in an old-fashioned Italian ice-cream parlour. Across the Bay of Naples, Vesuvius wore its white plume, while in the foreground there were cypresses, terraces, red roofs and tumbling bougain-villaea, and the sky was a joyous Neapolitan blue. For one reason, if not another, the panorama always bright-ened our ascent to bed. And, by way of throwing a perfume on the violet, the young artists had actually painted a banister upon the lower part of the view.

What happened when we had visitors was this. Our house guest would spend a convivial evening in town, in Gerry's Club or the Buckstone. At about 1 a.m. and hearing the discreet cough of a taxi motor, Honey would leave her bed, which was the foot of ours, and take up a position at the head of the stairs. The front door opened, a hall light clicked on, and the wassailer began to toil upwards. Often, seeing Honey staring at him he would say 'Hello, pussy-wussy' or make a pish-pish noise. Then, faced with the task of circumnavigating a small cat, he would steady himself by gripping one of the two banisters. It was, as any bookmaker would allow, an even-money bet chance that he would take hold of the painted one.

I am a sound sleeper. Only now and again did I hear the despairing cry as our house guest toppled backwards into the void. Whenever, because of the noise, I did come half-awake, there was always a few seconds of silence, then a gentle plop as Honey landed back on the coverlet, purring with the quiet contentment of a *tricoteuse* who has just seen off a vintage crop of *aristos*.

One evening, myself returning home with our particular friend, the actor David Kelly, I found Honey not at the stairhead but on a landing. She was crouched, and a glance told us that she was extremely ill.

'Ah, she's very sick,' Dave said, and a chill went through me. An Irishman will always soften bad news, so that a major coronary is no more than a 'bad turn' and a near-hurricane that leaves thousands homeless is 'good drying weather'. To describe a cat as very sick was virtually a sentence of death.

Even though she had had her injections as a kitten, Honey had caught enteritis. Thanks to our vet and Paule's devoted nursing, she pulled through, but remained a small cat, as if her growth had been arrested short of full size. A few weeks later, Dave, who was by now home in Dublin, telephoned. He beat a wide circle around the bush, then spiralled into the heart of it.

'The reason I rang up . . . ah, God, it's slipped my mind,' he lied. His voice became cotton wool. 'Ah, not meaning to bring up a sore . . . ah, whatsit, upset you, but the . . . ah, little cat . . . did she—'

'She's fine, Dave. She got better.'

There was a silence one could hear. Then, limp with relief, he said: 'She never did! Well, isn't she a right bad bugger?'

The nickname stuck. Thenceforth, Honey was the Bad Bugger. It is the same with pets as with children; we name them too early, then, when their true selves emerge, it is too late for change. The next-door neighbour's little boy, piously christened Francis Xavier, grows up to be a rabid atheist, just as their tortoiseshell, Cuddles, becomes a snarling blur of fang and claw. In Dave's terminology, a 'bad bugger' was a cat you relied upon to die, who then made a fool of you by staying alive. He has an upside-down kind of wit; once, when he was rehearsing for an Abbey Theatre production of Gorky's *The Lower Depths*, I asked him the play's running time. He told me 'Three hours,' then added: 'Two-and-a-half, with laughs.'

It was not long after Honey fell ill that Prissy began his infiltration campaign. Perhaps, aware that her life had been all but despaired of, he revised his plan of waiting for Miss King to die. An easy berth, soon to be without an occupant, could be his for the taking; it was then or never. He began to frequent our garden, which was the next but one to his own, and to cry plaintively and most humbly. Paule, of course, fell into his trap and would rush out with tidbits. *'Oh, comme elle est belle!'* she would croon (we still thought of him as female), whereupon his plume of a tail soared and his wails became little mews of gratitude.

He played his role well and without shame; no cat ever rubbed up more seductively against a leg. His visits became regular. Of a morning, he was to be seen on the sill of our garden-room window, seemingly awaiting our pleasure, but in reality awaiting his own. He did not seek to enter further than the doorstep; in that respect, he never overplayed his paw. And we, like fools, were grateful for his condescension.

'Priscilla,' Miss King said one day, 'seems to have adopted you. She never comes home to me at all.'

We protested that we had not meant to poach his affections. She smiled sadly and forgave us in a manner so saintly as to beget the later suspicion that she may have been relieved to see the last of him. There was a side of Prissy that was sheer Edward Hyde. For the present, however, there were the niceties to be observed, such as inviting him to grace our home. He stepped over the threshold in a courtly manner, like a Royal not embarrassing a cottager. Honey regarded him wearily from her sick-bed as if to say that having cat 'flu was surely bad enough on its own.

To be fair, I do Prissy's memory a disservice by comparing him with Mr Hyde. If you did not cross him, he had no qualms about permitting you to live. He reminded me, though, of one of those cats in gothic tales of terror in which reside an infinite capacity for vengeance. Fernand Mery wrote 'God made the cat in order that man might have the pleasure of caressing the tiger', and Prissy was a case in point. Most cats, if teased, will counter-attack with unsheathed claws; then, when the tormentor sues for peace, there is an armistice, or at least a truce. Not so with Prissy. If you belittled his dignity to the point, say, of rolling him on his back in the commonly-held delusion that it is people who play with cats rather than the other way about, then Armageddon was instant. It was as if a new and barbaric kind of weaponry had been released: a spring-mounted battery of steel knives, slashing upwards at the molesting hand. And if you at once withdrew and walked away, that would be victory enough for most cats. Prissy, however, would stalk after you, wrap his front paws around your leg and sink his small, exquisitely sharp teeth into the calf of the enclosed leg. He took no prisoners.

He became one of the family. He and Honey ignored each other; they might have been the tenants of two bed-sitters in Belfast, a Catholic and an Orangeman, who pass each other on the stairs, and are deterred from open war only by the presence of the landlord. Towards us humans, Priscilla now and again unbent to the extent of proffering his forehead for a circumspect stroking, but otherwise his contempt did not breed familiarity. One day, perhaps from overeating, he became more than usually liverish and was hauled off to the vet; and it was he who broke the news to my wife that Prissy was actually a chap. I felt a surge of affection; it excused much. My sympathy became an outright torrent when Paule went to fill the vet's prescription for tablets and saw that on it the cat's name had been written as 'Pissy'. The poor fellow's shame was complete. I would have given him a consolatory hug, had I dared.

Our menage was not quite complete, for by now and unbeknownst to us, Tinkle was waiting in the wings. He was a massive ginger tom with a leonine head. Someone had strung a small bell around his neck on a red ribbon to warn birds that he was in the offing; hence his name. His owners, a Scots family, had moved away from Barnes, unaccountably leaving him to fend for himself. Unlike Prissy, however, he lacked cunning; or perhaps, rather, he had too much pride. He did not impose himself. He would accept food, but not quite enough to keep from starving; we saw him on the common or the green, shivering under the lee of a fence, or wandering about, disconsolate, pining and homeless.

The day came when it was a case of surrender or die. He advanced to our back doorstep, lapped half-heartedly at a saucer of milk, then crouched instead of taking his leave. His whole aspect exuded misery. When he raised his head, we noticed that his inner eyelid – the nictitating membrane – had not retracted. It was a sure sign that he was ill. I stroked him, and he at once grasped my forefinger with a paw that was as deep and commodious as a baby's hand. (No other cat ever did that until – as I write – the other day when Panache, our Balinese kitten, followed in Tinkle's wake.) He purred – a massive throbbing that threatened to shake the walls. He had kept the faith; although deserted, he had been steadfast. Unlike Prissy, who was what Sean O'Casey would have called 'a slim-thinkin', go-be-the-wall', Tinkle's affections, slowly given, were lifelong.

In the three years that followed, the cats enjoyed an idyll. Prissy hunted, Tinkle pursued his amours, and Honey sat looking out at our rose garden and the great world beyond through a mullioned window. I have often put to myself the question: what is a cat *for*? This is as futile an exercise as asking what laughter is for. Say simply that back in 1966 a small girl asked for a pet, and, after twenty-six years of addiction, we have discovered that a house without tyrants is every bit as lonely as a house without angels. Probably the two are one and the same; at any rate, it took the whim of an Irish politician to inflict havoc upon the lives of our particular despots.

It was called the Haughey Scheme, and it applied to writers, artists and composers. It decreed that work of 'artistic and creative merit', would be free of income tax. The snag – or the blessing, according to taste – was that one was obliged to live and work in Ireland. I knew instantly that I must go home, not so that I might earn more but to make do with less. Henceforth, I would spend most of the year writing for the theatre. And, at the back of my head, I had always known that Ireland – a messy, begrudging, jeering, thin-skinned, dilatory, amoral, winking, apathetic, slanderous land with a philosophy of 'Ah sure, it'll do!' – was in spite of all, and perhaps because of all, my home, and that homes are for returning to.

We put our London house on the market and, after viewing a dozen mouldering villas, found a bungalow in Killiney a mile or so from Dalkey, where I had grown up. Our homecoming was unlikely to be the occasion for bunting along Castle Street – the mutters of 'tax sponger' reached all the way from the Dalkey pubs to the house in Barnes; happily, as George Moore observed, nothing lasts long in Ireland except the miles (an Irish mile goes on for 2,240 yards instead of the English 1,760). Our new home was high on an elbow of Killiney Hill. To the west, along the curve of Dublin Bay, was the city; whereas, to the south, we could see the Dublin and Wicklow Mountains, the two Sugar Loafs and Bray Head, and the sweep of the Vale of Shananagh, rimmed by the long crescent moon of Killiney strand. On a still night, one could hear the soft breathing of sea against sand. We had two and a half acres and a great sycamore – my first tree. Whatever about us – Paule, Danielle and me – it would be a cats' paradise. I could hardly wait for Honey, Prissy and Tinkle to see their new home.

We arranged our move for April, 1970. I am a great planner, and nothing was left to chance; the unforeseen simply did not have a leg to stand on. Then, with a few months still to go, a single case of feline rabies was diagnosed in the English midlands. The importation of all domestic animals to Ireland was at once proscribed by law.

The Perfect Crime

MY WIFE and I have always been law-abiding; she, because she is Belgian, whereas my own motive is the more universal one of cowardice. I need only see a police car in my rear-view mirror for my hands to go damp, and it is by a supreme act of will that I do not pull over to the verge, babbling that it is a fair cop.

As far as Prissy and Tinkle were concerned, it was clear that a home must be found for them until such time as the travel ban was lifted. Honey, though, was a case apart. She had never been further from the house than the small back garden, and there was not one chance in a million that she could be a carrier of infection. And she was delicate; none of us believed that she could survive many loveless months in a cattery. We talked, argued, and sat in haggard silence, but the decision was made and needed only to be given voice.

At last, I said: 'We'll have to smuggle her.'

'Oh, Jasus,' said my twelve-year-old daughter, whom we had encouraged to stay up late whenever Irish friends came to call.

Conscience did not enter into it; we were as callous as old lags. We simply could not leave the cat behind, and that was that. Our only qualms were to do with the very real fear of being caught. There was not a day when my ears did not echo to the imagined slam of Mountjoy Gaol's iron gates. Or, as I worked on a script, my mind's eye saw the airport customs hall, and I heard the cat come awake and betray us with a Judas miaow. At this, my heart would turn turtle like a coffin-ship in a Force Nine, and the rest of the day was lost.

Our plan, when fully formed, was an elegant creation, as meticulous as one of the better kinds of bank heist, and as daft. Its essence was that Honey would be carried, unconscious, into Ireland. The details followed each other as inescapably as the steps in Euclid that lead to the great Q.E.F.

First, if the cat was to be kept sedated, it followed that a long trip overland and by sea was out of the question. So Paule – I can still hear her whimperings of terror – and Danielle would travel by air, with Honey drugged and asleep in an overnight bag, while I imported our car through Liverpool.

Second, flying direct to Dublin was asking for trouble. Passengers from Britain were obliged to run a gauntlet of customs officers, who – the bad old days were as yet not over with – were still on the lookout for such milestones of pornography as Joyce's *Stephen Hero* and *The Catcher in the Rye*. There was, however, no such hurdle in Belfast, which was part of the United Kingdom; and the security checks that came with the Northern troubles were still a year or so in the future. Barring miaowings from the interior of a travel bag, one would simply walk through. And so another piece of the plan clicked into shape; the three of them – two awake, one sleeping – would fly into Northern Ireland and from there catch a train for Dublin.

Third, the criminals had need of an accomplice.

We had not far to look. Vernon (or so I shall call him) lived next door to us. He was an actor and the perfect neighbour: kindly and cheery, and he was a lover of cats, including ours. Whenever my wife went visiting her relatives in Liège, he saw to it that I did not go native. Knowing that I could be trusted to feed the cats, but not myself, he cooked dinner for us both. He had lived alone since the death of his close friend, Geoffrey. He was Welsh but, happily, he did not sing. Instead, on two evenings each week, he went to see a spiritualist in the hope of making contact with the departed. Lately, he told me, the portents had been good. At a séance, a medium had uttered the tag-line of a private joke between Geoffrey and himself. He took heart; a breakthrough was not far off.

When we told him of our plan to smuggle Honey into Ireland, he not only agreed to help, but was enraptured. It was his first cloak-and-dagger role, ever. He took to coming into our house after dark by flattening himself against the outside wall and then darting in silently, like Peter Lorre carrying letters of transit.

Our plan was watertight, except for two imponderables. The first was that the flight to Belfast might be delayed, giving the cat time to come to, perhaps in mid-journey; the second was that the cat might come to, even if the flight were on time. 'That's a chance,' I said stoutly, 'that we'll have to take.' At the 'we', I knew that my wife was looking at me, but I was not such a fool as to meet her eye.

As for the plan itself, it was never committed to paper, but we all knew the timetable by heart. It went as follows.

8.30 a.m. Arrival of removals men, who would load our household effects into a container for conveying to Dublin.

1.00 p.m. I leave for Liverpool to ship our car across.

1.15 p.m. Removals men depart. Paule and Vernon

take the cat to a vet, who has been conned into believing that Honey is going eastwards to Brussels instead of illicitly to Ireland.

2.45 p.m. Paule and Danielle check in with doped cat at Heathrow.

3.15 p.m. Flight time to Belfast.

4.45 p.m. Arrive Aldergrove Airport. By taxi to Victoria Station.

6 p.m. By *Enterprise* express to Amiens Street Station, Dublin, where a friend is waiting with a cat tray, a pooper-scooper and a bag of litter.

8.30 p.m. Check in at Hibernian Hotel and have nervous breakdown.

On H (for Honey)-Day minus one, we left Prissy and Tinkle with a hearty lady who owned a cattery near Datchet. Over coffee, she told us about an American client who arrived by hired car, having driven it from London in first gear while under the impression that, like her Chevvy back home, it was an automatic. She delivered the punch line by giving her tweedy thigh a slap that rang out like a rifle-shot in an autumn wood. In reply, we could muster only the faintest of smiles; we were brooding on the morrow. She must have thought us heartless; so distraught were we at the ordeal ahead that we merely nodded our farewell to her two new boarders. The same thought had occurred to us both: this was a nice cattery. Honey would have been happy here; instead, and thanks to us, she would probably end up repining in the gaol that was quarantine. Never had folly seemed so foolish.

Next morning, the removals men came. At one o'clock, on schedule, I thanked Vernon for his assistance and kissed my wife and child goodbye, wondering where, when and if I would see them again, then set off towards the M1. As for Honey's journey to Dublin, it proved to be a story with a twist in the tail.

First, Vernon brought her to the vet, who injected her. He told Paule that there was nothing to worry about; the cat would sleep for four or five hours, and, for as long as her tongue was visibly protruding, she would be comfortably 'under'.

Honey was tenderly placed in a travel bag provided by Vernon and tucked in as snugly as a baby in its cot. More goodbyes were said, and Paule and Danielle set off by taxi for Heathrow. A glance at the departures board told them that their flight would leave on time. They sat, waiting to be called.

Dan peered into the travel bag.

'Mum, Honey's tongue is in.'

'What?'

'I can't see it.'

'Oh, Jasus.' (My Liègoise wife, like Danielle, had had her life and vocabulary enriched by an acquaintance with Irish actors.) It was true; there was not a sign of the small, pink tongue.

I do not know what Paule hoped to achieve by what she then attempted. If a cat's tongue is protruding, it may very well be proof that the animal is unconscious (there are more things in heaven and earth, etc); but the reverse does not necessarily apply. It is not axiomatic that by grasping the tongue and pulling it into the light of day one will at once induce a small coma. Nonetheless, my wife reached into the bag, took hold of the recalcitrant tongue and gave it a gentle tug.

At this, Honey opened a watery eye and sank a fang deep into the ball of Paule's thumb.

Blood began to well up. Danielle, who shares my passion for old films, says that it was just like the bubbling of the miraculous source in *The Song of Bernadette*. The bleeding was generous, and it refused to stop. Paule, conscious that at any moment other passengers would take notice or, worse, an airport official might come to her assistance, suppressed an urge to behave like a newly headless hen. With a hiss of 'Call the vet!', she fled towards the ladies' lavatory.

Our daughter, left alone, looked into the travel bag. Honey, her tongue back where it belonged, seemed to be again at peace. Dan lugged the bag to a telephone and dialled the vet's number. He heard her out and chuckled. No problem; the cat was simply not as heavily doped as had been intended. All, he told her, was well. Danielle hung up and said another word much favoured by Irish actors.

Meanwhile, Paule found the ladies' lavatory to be too crowded for comfort. Again fearful of attracting attention, she locked herself in a cubicle where she knelt, put her wounded hand in the toilet bowl, shut her eyes and pulled the chain. It took five minutes and as many flushes for the stream of blood to dwindle to the merest rill; then, with her hand swathed in toilet paper, Paule returned to the departure lounge to learn from Dan that Honey did not so much sleep as cat-nap.

Their flight was called; they boarded; they took off. It is my wife's impression to this day that the journey from Heathrow to Aldergrove lasted all of seven hours. The travel bag – it was their only baggage – was between Dan's feet, and now and again she felt it twitch, as if with the unease of a sleeper having a restless night.

They landed. It is quite one thing to walk past the scrutiny of customs officers, who are as armed sentries manning a frontier. Entering an unstaffed arrivals hall is more like traversing a minefield; you wait for the emptiness to erupt: in this case the voice that says: 'A moment, if you please, madam.' Paule and Dan walked on legs that threatened to fail; they saw a door marked 'Taxis'; they just succeeded not to run. They were through.

An hour later, they were on the *Enterprise*, bound nonstop for Dublin. The ban on importing cats did not exist between Northern Ireland and Eire, if only for the very good reason that with a hundred miles of unapproved border roads no one could hope to enforce it. Honey was, by the way, an intelligent cat; she knew the danger was past, and the train had not even reached the no-man's-land of Slieve Gullion before she began to celebrate in bel canto.

No, this is whimsy; for all I know, her song may have been less paean than dirge. She may have been complaining that all in the one day she had been per- forated by a needle, had her tongue rudely pulled and had been obliged to travel by taxi, airplane, taxi again and, now, train. For the homeward-bound business men who packed the long carriage it was much of a muchness; to the untrained ear there is, after all, little to choose between the Siamese version of the Hallelujah chorus and the Irish lament known as *An Cúilín*. As rendered, all that they had in common was carrying power, and Honey in full voice could be heard back in the guard's van.

The performance began as the *Enterprise* traversed the high ridge to the west of Newry. At first, it was a soft, insistent wailing that made a few of the passengers look about them for a concealed baby. By Dundalk, the first town past the border, the cry was accompanied by a kind of contrapuntal growling. Also, the volume had been turned up a couple of notches. By Drogheda, Honey had found her pitch and was in fine spate, with a full-blooded yowl audible even to the severed head of the martyred Oliver Plunkett on his side altar in West Street. Dublin was only another thirty miles, but it was too far for some. The noise was the aural equivalent of a kidney stone; it was not the discord that was maddening, but the monotony; it did not vary or promise to fall away; it was tireless.

At Amiens Street, the carriage emptied like an upturned water jug. Paule and Dan were among the last off the train and could see our Irish friend waiting just beyond the customs barrier and endeavouring to look as if a plastic tray and a bag of cat litter were as much a part of his daily impedimenta as a fountain pen in his handkerchief pocket, and the *Irish Times*. At the barrier, Honey rounded off her concert with a thrilling flourish. The female customs official peered inside the bag.

She smiled at Paule and Danielle. 'What a lovely little pussy cat.'

By this time, I was sitting in a raffish quayside pub in Liverpool, waiting to board the B. and I. ferry. There was nothing to read but a fragment of the *Daily Mirror* a customer had left behind. I remember that, having twice pored over every word, I began in desperation to

play anagrams. When at last drivers were admitted to the car deck, I found a pay telephone and called the Royal Hibernian Hotel. I asked to be put through to my wife's room and waited, wondering how long I could hold my breath. The voice that answered belonged to our friend, Phyllis Ryan, who every year produced a play of mine at the Dublin Theatre Festival. Like Vernon in London, Phyllis had a love of cloak-and-dagger.

She said: 'They're safe and sound,' and added, cryptically: 'And the parcel is with them.'

When I had spoken with my wife, who was in a state of delayed shock, I hung up and, as an afterthought called the hotel again, this time to speak to one of the receptionists.

'I wanted to tell you,' I said, 'that my daughter in Room 210 has a kitten with her.' (It sounded less of an enormity than saying 'cat'.) 'I trust this is permitted?'

'No problem at all, sir,' the girl said. 'We'll pop it into the fridge.'

She hung up, and it was not until next day that I learned she had misheard me and was under the impression that Danielle was travelling with a chicken. The Hibernian is gone now, and I miss it dearly.

I have said that the story has a twist in the tail. At 7.30 next morning, this exile arrived home. It was a clear April morning, hard with sunlight. Ireland was welcoming me like an old girl friend, in need of more lipstick now and winking from a doorstep. I drove into town, parked in Molesworth Street and crossed to the Hibernian. There was a joyous family reunion, not much entered into by the cause of it all, who was still under the influence and tottering about the bedroom like a drunk. Otherwise, Honey was none the worse for her odyssey, and it occured to me that we should call Vernon and tell him that crime in this instance did pay.

His voice came on the line.

'Vernon, all's well. We—'

He did not allow me to finish. He said: 'Yes, I knew it would be. I went to a spiritualist friend to ask a blessing on the journey, and she said that the lady would get there safely, but would be badly bitten on the left hand. Did it happen?'

I said: 'Would you mind repeating that?' and passed the receiver to Paule.

If you are going to dine out on a tall tale for ever afterwards, it is good to have a witness.

*   *   *

Writers cannibalize everyone, even themselves, and Honey's story seemed made to measure for a television play. I had already written five plays for Armchair Theatre, a series which in the 1960s pioneered the work of Alun Owen, Clive Exton, and Robert Muller. If it was not a golden age, it was at least gold-plated. Plays had by then ceased to be transmitted live, but no one really knew how to edit video-tape so they were recorded in three parts without a pause. In consequence, what went wrong stayed wrong, and the drama on the screen was as nothing compared with that upstairs in the 'box', where the director called his shots.

The creative genius of Armchair Theatre was a Canadian, Sidney Newman, who was affectionately known as El Sid. In later years he went to the BBC and thence to the film company, Associated British, and I remember with affection our last professional contact. He was anxious to make a film of a television play of mine named *Silent Song*, which was set in a Trappist monastery and was virtually without dialogue. 'What we need,' he had said in broaching the subject, 'is to find the missing ingredient – the love interest.'

We met at the studios for lunch. 'Wait till you hear who I've got lined up,' El Sid told me. 'Whaddya say to Bob Hope and Bing Crosby?'

We were eating liver and bacon, and I was conscious that a piece of rind was hanging limply over my lower lip as I stared at him. He added with the wistfulness of a man whose ideals are forever thwarted: 'I suppose *The Road to Calvary* is a bit sick?'

The film was never made, but at least Sidney always thought big. And in his Armchair Theatre days he had assembled a team of talented play directors. Ted Kotch-eff and Silvio Narizzano came from Canada; others, like Alan Bridges and Philip Saville, were home-grown. Among the latter was an ex-actor named Guy Verney. He was a journeyman director, rather than a critics' darling, but he had a flair for comedy and enjoyed working with Irish actors, whom he indulged rather in the benign manner of the white interlocutor in a Christy Minstrels show. He looked forward to directing *Sweeney*, as I called the play-to-be.

I have a picture postcard he sent me. It shows the Gayer Anderson Egyptian cat in the British Museum. The wording goes: *Glad to hear 'Sweeney' is now all signed and sealed. Arrive Dublin on Saturday 10.35 a.m. by BE 914, unless we are hi-jacked by the I.R.A. G.V.*

He had given no previous indication that he was coming to Dublin. It was unlike him to rise to the expense of a private visit, and ABC Television did not fly their directors abroad to discuss scripts that were as yet unwritten. At short notice, I rounded up every Irish actor who had ever worked with Guy, and on the Sunday evening we threw a party in his honour. He had an unabashed, almost feminine vanity that was beguiling to see. As the still centre of attention, he had a splendid time.

When the last guest had gone home, Guy and I had a final drink to soften the violence of sobering up, a process that should be done under the anaesthetic of sleep. He sat in my swivel chair, and Honey climbed on his lap as if it were a casting couch. It was a summer night and there was already a lightening sky beyond the Kish lighthouse to the east. We had not yet discussed the script. I told him that I knew the starting point of my journey and its end; the road between was, as always with me, a mist that would lift as I wrote.

He was not in the least interested. One hand stroked Honey and the other made a small, vaguely Royal-Family, gesture. He said: 'I know your methods, Holmes.'

'Then—' I paused. Guy was prickly when sober; with gin and tonic lapping at his back teeth, he was a human cactus. I said, picking my steps: 'Not that we aren't thrilled to see you, but if the script didn't bring you here, what did?'

He looked at me as if I were out of focus. 'I don't know.' Then he waved again to the populace. 'A whim.'

He went home next day. He was punctilious about sending – and receiving – thank-you notes, and when I had not heard from him by mid-week, a faint foreboding began to stir. On the Saturday morning, a friend called to say that Guy, who was in his fifties, had had a stroke soon after his return home. I called his Twickenham number at once and was told that he had died earlier that day.

Honey's play was never written. Without Guy, it wouldn't have been the same.

The Boys

'THE BOYS' was our nickname for the absent Tinkle and Priscilla. We received the occasional progress report from the lady who owned the cattery near Datchet; Tinkle, she said, was a city boy and found the passing glimpses of wild life a constant marvel. In particular, he was fascinated by a pheasant that regularly strolled about outside his enclosure.

Meanwhile, Honey was settling into her new home three hundred miles away. Like Tinkle, she discovered much of local interest. There were, for example, the seagulls, which provoked her to emit a *kek-kek-kek* of pure hatred. The *pièce de résistance*, however, was Mr O'Brien, who mowed our acre and a half of lawn and

planted a shrub or two in the borders. He might have
been a dissolute fifty or a virginal seventy-five; he had
a white face as flat as a headstone and wore a residual
scowl and a wig that resembled a hirsute tea cosy. Our
garden was on a slope, and Honey looked on without
comment as Mr O'Brien pursued the motor mower
downhill at a crooked run and rheumatically urged it
back up again. She was careful to stay out of his way;
he was a countryman and looked upon the keeping of
pets, other than sheepdogs, as a frivolity.

Jobbing gardeners were as rare as hens' teeth, and
we had obtained Mr O'Brien by a cynical appeal to his
baser nature. My wife has always disliked my pen
name, which began as a joke played on the Abbey
Theatre and thereafter hung about my neck like
Sinbad's Old Man of the Sea. Having married a civil
servant named Jack Keyes Byrne, she felt ill-done-by at
finding herself the wife of a writer named Hugh
Leonard; it savoured of having been pitchforked into a
ménage à trois. It was no good for me to protest that
Hugh Leonard existed not at all as a person, but only
as two words on the title page of a playscript; she had
the aggrievedness of a woman who has ordered rice
pudding and been given apple crumble. To make it
worse, Ireland is so hard up for celebrities that it wildly
over-uses the few it has, and, as far as her treasured
privacy was concerned, I was as much a local landmark

as the proverbial begging ass. With Mr O'Brien, Paule broke her own rule; she answered his advertisement, signing herself Mrs Leonard in the hope that he would be unable to resist a glimpse of the excesses of *la vie bohème*.

In the Ireland of the 1970s the swinging '60s had gone missing, presumed lost, *en route* from Holyhead. In our town there were rumours of wife-swapping on Wyatt-ville Road beyond in Ballybrack, but no one had been quite able to pin it down. This only lent force to the suspicion that the entire country was riddled with secret vice, and that the haves had closed ranks against the have-nots. At any rate, Mr O'Brien took the bait, came to us and was disappointed. 'I might as well,' Paule said to me, 'get some good out of that bloody name.'

Honey was unfazed by the removal to Ireland, where she began her new life by disdaining a famous knee. I had sent out change-of-address cards, and one of these brought a cabled reply from Vevey in Switzerland: 'REMOVAL FROM BARNES TO DUBLIN EMINENTLY SENSIBLE STOP WILL BE YOUR FIRST GUEST STOP ARRIVING SATURDAY JAMES.' The sender was the actor, James Mason, with whom I had worked on a projected film version of *Jane Eyre*, to star himself as Rochester, with Rita Tushingham as Jane. Like all the best films, it was never to happen, but our few days together had resulted in a friendship. Throughout my cinema-mad twenties, the two film stars I most admired were James Mason and the Canadian actor, Alexander Knox; it was part of my absurd good fortune that less than two decades later both of them became my friends.

James, as promised, arrived on the Saturday. His addiction to cats was world-famous, which may have been why Honey ignored his lap in the fastidious manner of a woman of virtue preferring not to consort with a known philanderer. While James, without pre-amble, launched into a monologue, she sat on the window sill and looked out at the Dublin Mountains.

I had never known him to be loquacious; as a York-shireman, he had always been frugal with words, doling out, as from a purse, not one more than the occasion required. The reason for his trip to Ireland was as spokesman for a concern that was a forerunner of the Friends of the Earth; he sat amid our unpacked tea-chests and threw out facts and figures as if by rote, while Paule and I nodded with an affectation of deep absorption. That evening, we saw him being inter-viewed on *The Late Late Show*, and he delivered the same speech word for word. I realized then that we had been his guinea pigs; or rather, as the expression goes, he had been trying it on the dog. Certainly, the cat was not in the least interested.

Later, I wondered if he had ever really been a cat

person or if, like his reputation for rudeness, it was one more fiction of the image industry. There is a story, *Jane*, by Somerset Maugham in which the heroine earns a reputation as a great wit simply because, amid the brittleness of Mayfair society, she tells the truth. In the same way, James's habit of answering a question with simple directness was perceived to be a kind of brutality.

He was shy and, if faced down, could take fright. One Sunday afternoon, he proposed himself as my guide on a stroll that turned into a murderous hike over the hills behind Vevey. The soles of my city shoes registered the shape of every pebble on the road, and I was glad of the respite when he stopped to admire a clump of long-stemmed wayside flowers. 'These are jolly,' he said and picked an armful, whereupon a fat woman came charging out of a nearby cottage with a hoarse cry of '*Monsieur, c'est defendu!*' She was closely followed by two young men who, to judge from their circumference, were probably her sons. James did not wait to apologize; neither did he surrender his loot. Instead, he thrust the flowers into my arms and took to his heels. Tired as I was from walking, I was inspired to follow him at a kind of galumphing run.

A passing photographer could have had a field day. With Lake Geneva in the background, one of the world's darlings, aged fifty, was in head-long flight, followed by a forty-year-old Irish playwright with an

armful of stolen flowers, pursued in turn by an avalanche of two boulder-like Switzers and their mother.

After a time, I found myself alone. James, who
believed in physical fitness, had disappeared around a
bend in the hillside, and the others had abandoned the
chase. I paused, took a deep breath of pure Swiss air,
and heard a wheeze, as of a very old bedspring. After
a time, I resumed walking and, not more than a mile
or so further on, saw James sitting in his car; our hike-
cum-run had brought us full circle to the starting point.

The look on my face must have been murderous, for
before I could speak he threw me a *bon-bon*. 'Did I
mention we're having dinner with Charlie and Oona
this evening?' he said winsomely.

I was not to be bought off, even with an evening *chez*
Chaplin, and in any case I had always preferred Laurel
and Hardy.

'Here, Mason,' I said, 'are your ****ing flowers,' (the
asterisks denote a word not usually found in cat books),
all but shoving them in his face. Our friendship dated,
I think, from that moment.

When James died, his wife, Clarissa Kaye, described
him as a saint. I am inclined to agree with her, and it
would be all the nicer if the mythology was for once
true and he really was a lover of cats.

* * *

Six months after our arrival in Ireland, the importation ban was lifted. The lady from Datchet met me at Heathrow, and I took delivery of two wickerwork baskets that meowed at me all the way to the Aer Lingus check-in. Prissy and Tinkle duly came home by air and, by the way, lost a life apiece in the process. They had of course travelled in the hold, and, with the journey over, I stood in the baggage area at Dublin Airport, and watched the conveyor belt judder into life. Perhaps from a vague anxiety, I went and lifted one of the leather flaps through which the baggage came wobbling into view like prizes in a television games show. What I saw was the two baskets being flung any-which-way off a trolley and at once disappearing under a mountain of what looked like steamer trunks, with more to come.

I yelled something on the lines of: 'For God's sake, you'll crush those animals.'

One of the baggage-handlers said: 'Yah wha'?'

'There are cats in those baskets. You'll squash them.'

A pause. Then the reply came: 'The public is not allowed to trick-act with them yokes.' He meant the leather flaps.

In this way, face had been saved, so I stood back, and moments later sure enough, the baskets came safely through, each with two anxious cat-eyes visible at the small window. A great sentimental 'Awww!' went up from my fellow-passengers. Meanwhile, I had overheard a colloquy from the baggage handlers at the far side of the flaps.

'That's your man.'

'Who?'

'You know . . . your man.' (Locally, 'your man' is a form of emphasis which has the same effect as pointing a finger, but requires not so much exertion.)

'Whoever he is, he's ****in'´particular.' (The asterisks fulfil the same purpose as heretofore.)

'Him? Look at him crossways and he'd hang you.'

'Jasus. Well, the get.' (Dublinese for 'misbegotten').

'Oh, a notorious bollix.'

This, in a Dublin context, was not calumny or even invective; it was small talk, and no offence could possibly be taken. I conveyed Tinkle and Prissy home to Killiney, where they remained to the end of their days.

Prissy had not enjoyed the vicissitudes of travel, nor had the sojourn in Datchet lent sweetness to his nature. He was no sooner out of the basket than, ignoring the doting cries from Paule and Danielle, he identified the author – as he thought – of his woes and bit him (me) in the leg. As for Tinkle, there was, in the beginning, a problem with his libido. Unlike Prissy, he had not been neutered at the onset of puberty, and his months of enforced celibacy had made him impatient to be out and doing. Paule and I agreed that he should be kept indoors for at least ten days to inure him to his new

surroundings. Tinkle begged to differ. After no more than two days in his new home, ennui overcame him and he slipped out through an unguarded back door.

Ours was the first bungalow on a new estate that had once been the grounds of Park House. It was a familiar story; what had been a home of the Quality was reduced first to hard times and then to rubble; and then, although the word had not yet been minted, the yuppies moved in. Our estate was grandly christened Killiney Heath, but with the Irish genius for sobriquet it became known locally as Disneyland. At the time we moved in, Park House was still standing – grey, empty and awaiting its end – and there was open land rolling towards Ballybrack a half-mile away. Tinkle, his eyes besotted by distance, set off at a prowl, his great head arcing from side to side as if the lawn were a minefield and he a detector. I made an out-flanking manoeuvre and tried to shoo him back to the house.

If love is blind, so perhaps is lust, and for all the attention he paid, I might have been a pile of builders' rubble or the foot-high garden fence he stepped over, a massive paw at a time. I looked about for a stick, but could find only a length of barbed wire to wave at him, not as a weapon but as a kind of empty threat. This was unwise; Tinkle was not only a London cat, but probably an Eastender.

He looked at the barbed wire and frowned. I had not

seen a cat frown before, but a cat did so now. He spat
at the wire, then looked along its length to my arm,
and from there up to my shoulder and beyond, until
his eyes locked with mine. He snarled and backed off,
not in retreat but crouching for a spring. My nerve
broke; I threw the barbed wire away, in the manner of
a cornered gangster dropping his .38, and gave Tinkle
his road. My wife was watching from a window, and
the last we saw of him was his ginger tail: a swaying
cobra in the long grass. 'Well,' I said, 'that's the last
we'll see of him.'

He came back six days later, not scowling but smiling.

* * *

To live in Killiney Heath was to bear witness to the end
of an age. We had not willingly bought the bungalow,
but it was the only alternative to the millstone of what
in estate agent's jargon was described as a 'gentleman's
residence', with the often added and ominous euphem-
ism 'in need of some repair'.

We were shown one such place on Ardbrugh Road
in Dalkey. It had a free-standing granite outhouse that
was so crammed with the empty sherry and port bottles
of half a century that the only way to remove them
would be to knock down the four walls. The house
itself, crumbling to its grave, was littered with half-
completed jigsaw puzzles – I was reminded of Xanadu

in *Citizen Kane* – and in the kitchen I saw a very old woman wrapped in blue woollens and asleep at the table. She was certainly in her nineties, and an empty sherry schooner was in front of her.

'Is she one of the family?' I whispered to the estate agent who was showing us around.

'Actually, no,' he said. 'She's the maid.'

And so, *faute de mieux*, we bought the bungalow. Our neighbours were to include a restaurateur, an Ayckbourn-archetypal land 'developer' who gave vicars-and-tarts parties, and a show business impresario whose wife always left her wardrobe doors ajar so that visitors might marvel at the contents. In a rare unscabrous moment, Brendan Behan once defined an Anglo-Irishman as 'a Protestant on a horse'; in the same vein, an Irish business executive might be described as a Catholic on the make.

I was not aware then that I had come home to find a revolution in the making. Whereas the demise of the Big House had been a literary cliché for more than a generation, the nature of the society that would take its place was less clear. Perhaps because it was happening all about us, it took time to realize that we were in at the dawn of the Age of the Cute Whoor. 'Cute' in Ireland does not mean charming or quaint – rather, it describes a flair for skullduggery, and 'whoor' need not apply to the female of the species. When brought together, the two words denote a knavish businessman or politician, or perhaps both in one, who is too cunning to be found out. The irony of the Haughey Scheme was that it had enabled me to return to the Ireland of my youth in time to be a mourner at its wake.

At any rate, our neighbours in Disneyland were not our kind of people any more than we were theirs. We were too raffish for them; we longed for Dalkey where I grew up, a mile away by road or a light year as the crow flies. We made one friend, however: a dreadnought lady named Mairéad Andrews who lived at Druid Hill down the way. She had family connections with West's of Grafton Street and was a frequent visitor to Park House from heyday to decline.

'You know it's haunted, of course?' she told us.

The ghost's name was Etty; she was a gentle, frail creature whom Mrs Andrews had seen on several occasions. 'I do worry about what's to become of her,' she said, 'once those vandals tear the house down.'

For all her daunting appearance, our friend was golden-hearted. On the day that the house was bulldozed to the ground, she waited for the dust to settle, and at twilight I saw her roaming over the stones.

'Looking for a souvenir?' I asked.

She shook her head. 'I was asking Etty,' she said, 'if she would like to come and live with me.'

It was a kindly thought, but the offer was declined.

Perhaps, like certain wines, ghosts do not travel well.

Honey, Prissy and Tinkle enjoyed life on Killiney Heath, as far as a cat can stoop to the indignity of outright enjoyment. They were unaware of the great events of the day, and they watched with unconcern as I went down to the corner each morning to make my telephone calls. We were on the Post Office waiting list for six months, and my contacts with the outside world were either by letter, telegram or the pay call-box in the hallway of a nearby block of flats.

One day, thieves went to work and removed not only the contents of the coin box but the box itself. They were either compassionate or remiss, for the telephone still worked, except that coins, when inserted at the top end, now came tumbling out at the other. All calls were thus free of charge, and before long a Killiney Galileo or perhaps a Ballybrack Brunel hit upon the idea of putting a cardboard box on the floor to catch the cataract of copper and silver. The fame of the telephone spread locally, and often I would have to join a queue while those ahead of me, their pockets and purses stuffed with shillings, rang up their dear ones in Toronto, Cincinatti and Sydney.

I had a workroom in the garden where I wrote plays and did a little journalism by way of making mischief. On autumn nights, winds swept down from the Dublin mountains so that my reflection in the window plate-glass became concave and shook until work was impossible and I fled towards bed. In summer, I stayed up until first light; our sycamore tree and I had the world to ourselves. On the whole, life went smoothly apart from the occasional letter, always anonymous, from admirers of the Provisional I.R.A. It was an organisation I took pleasure in baiting at a time when Mr Haughey, his apostles and several bishops still regarded its members as a band of jovial rogues whose spiritual home was an Irish equivalent of Sherwood Forest.

Honey, Prissy and Tinkle continued to be indifferent to the world about them, but I think they looked forward to Christmas. This was because friends and their children would arrive in the afternoon, and the mere sight of a cat unfailingly turned the mother of the family into a trembling blancmange.

It is beyond dispute that if there are ten people in a room and only one of them is an ailurophobe, that person's lap is the one a cat will unerringly head for. No one knows why. Perhaps, the reason is simply that, like Everest, the lap is there.

It is wrong to think that a cat does not care whether you dislike it or not. A woman of beauty will walk into a restaurant or down the aisle of a theatre knowing, without seeming to look, whose head does not turn at her passing. She is like the archetypal actor who may receive a hundred admiring notices, and yet will take to heart only the single bad one. A cat is similarly an elegant, intuitive, self-obsessed female (whatever its sex); it instinctively knows its public from its critics. If you fail to accept it at its own valuation, retribution is swift. Honey, Prissy and Tinkle did not jump on our friend's lap; they were too subtle for frontal attack. They merely sat and looked at her.

'Your cats,' she would say with jollity, although her voice was soprano, 'are great friends.'

They looked at her with contempt, knowing that cats are not friends of other cats; they are their accomplices.

'If you are spared,' they were telling her, 'it is not by your merits but our whim.'

As for me, the only fault that all cats have in common is that they *will* die. Prissy was the first to go, the result of a bladder obstruction. He could, when he chose, be such an unyielding adversary that it seemed unsporting to have to take him to the vet.

Tinkle had a sadder fate, and it was our fault. With age, he had begun to lose his battles. He came home from the amatory lists with ears like torn pennants and wounds that would not heal, and we decided, too late, on what should have been done in the beginning. He was neutered, and, like Othello with his occupation gone, he lost the will to live. He went out one evening and this time never came back. Years later, a neighbour mentioned that he had found him in a sack of grain into which he had crawled to die.

In answer to my unasked question, he said: 'Sure there was no sense in upsetting you.'

It is only fair to suggest that there may have been another contributory cause of Tinkle's end. Its name was Rover.

Rover

MARMALADE CATS are nearly always males; Rover, however, had the distinction of being marmalade on his mother's side, paternity unknown. He was an orange blob no bigger than Paule's hand when he came to us in a shoebox that could have held six of him. A friend of a friend of ours urgently wanted a home for a male kitten; when we protested that he was not yet weaned, we were given to understand that his alternative home would be a weighted sack thrown over the sea wall. And so the shoebox changed hands.

By Rover's appearance, he might have been one of Tinkle's progeny, and possibly he was; the area over which that great amorist distributed his favours would not have disgraced an outback flying doctor. The premature change to solid food made the kitten sickly to begin with; he made up for this by living for fifteen happy (if one excepted a particular nine days) years, and attaining a gross (I use the word deliberately) weight of eighteen pounds.

On the evening of his arrival, Paule, Danielle and I sat and attempted to find a name for him. It was our daughter, by now a classics student at Trinity College, who brightly suggested 'Rover'. One could make the jibe that this was an example of undergraduate wit, but it was exactly the kind of name I myself would have chosen had I thought of it first – and I never went to university. There is a flaw in reasoning here, but let it pass.

In moments of fantasy, I have wondered if the choice of name had a traumatic effect on Rover, for, once he had cast off his kittenhood, he was the most uncattish cat imaginable. In the early days, however, he gambolled with the newly-gelded Tinkle, who was too old and dispirited to gambol in return. He no longer had an incentive for outdoor sports, and indoors there was no hiding place. The kitten, ready for play, would track him down, then wrestle, pounce, make bread on his back and swing from his tattered ears, and Tinkle, with paws that were each as big as his tormentor's head, was too good-natured to lash out. If Rover did not hasten the poor fellow's end, neither did he long delay it.

As for Honey, she detested the newcomer. Rover was both an interloper and a member of the lower orders (Siamese cats are the most incorrigible of snobs), and she would punish the merest suggestion of *lèse majesté* with a bite or the sabre-swipe of a paw whenever it seemed that no one was looking. The effect was that Rover, with affection to spare, lavished all of it on the benighted Tinkle. It was only when he grew to Honey's size and beyond it that there was a sullen armistice.

It was about this time that we became disaffected with Killiney Heath and moved house around the corner of the bay to Dalkey, which was not so much *nouveau riche* as comfortably *nouveau bourgeoise*. From there, Danielle would find it easier to catch a train into town each morning of term. Also, I had received a letter from a member of the local Quality on Killiney Hill Road, hailing me as a fellow parishioner and declaring that as such I was eligible to contribute £200 towards the cost of a new church organ. The fact that in seven years we had never been invited inside the writer's front gate mitigated the pain of endistancing ourselves from our betters. As for the £200, while not describing myself as an agnostic, I do not share the view popularly held by Irish Catholics that, to use their vernacular, they have a great leg of the Sacred Heart. So, as far as the church organ was concerned, I invited my neighbour to go fish.

The new house was actually three 150-year-old fishermen's cottages with an ugly modern bit tacked on at the front. It was a few yards away from Coliemore, a tiny medieval harbour that had once been known as the port of the Archbishop of Dublin. There, on a wild October night when I was ten, I almost drowned while attempting to save our dog, who was contriving to swim with a concrete block tied around his neck. My father hauled me out of the water and was so carried away by his heroism that he awarded himself a bar to his V.C. by rescuing the dog as well, quite forgetting that it was he who had thrown it into the harbour in the first place.

Our front windows faced across to Dalkey Island with its ruined church of St Begnet and the Martello Tower that is still on the lookout for Napoleon. The name Dalkey comes from the Norse *dalk-ei*, meaning Thorn Island. There is not a bush or tree on it; the 'thorns' were the pointed stakes used as palisades against the Vikings.

As far as Honey and Rover were concerned – Tinkle had by now gone to cat heaven – the only drawback of the new house was the motor traffic on the road between us and the foreshore. Honey, however, was a stay-at-home, and Rover could take care of himself. I had found that out on the night of a Killiney cloudburst. He had gone out for his constitutional, and it seemed impossible that any cat could survive when the steep hill roads turned to torrents. At first, I took the car out and drove about the district straining for a sight of him. Then I went on foot, calling his name into the downpour. As I returned home, catless and soaked, the storm ended. Five minutes later, he ambled in, as dry as a bone.

Until our removal to Dalkey, Rover had never been in a two-storey house. Now, once the ground floor had yielded its pleasures, he set his mind on higher things and started upstairs, taking his time. On the fifth step, I saw him stumble and trip.

It was impossible, but there it was: a cat had fallen over his own feet. One might more naturally expect Lester Piggot to mount a horse backwards or hear that the Pope had crossed himself the wrong way round. I saw Rover give exactly the same performance on two other occasions, but always I was the only witness.

'Our cat trips when going upstairs,' I said to a lady next to whom I was seated at dinner.

'Does he?' she replied. 'Isn't he great?'

She gave me a smile. It was a smile that said that liars are everywhere, that social intercourse would wither and die if they were not, and that a woman's most precious social gift is to affect to believe whatever nonsense she hears. Most of all, it was a smile that told me to pull the other one.

Rover's repertoire was not confined to having four left feet when climbing a flight of stairs. Our kitchen was bisected by a high formica-topped counter on which from time to time he would lie, the better to keep an eye on the preparation of his *plat du jour*. Often, he would enjoy a catnap, and one day I saw him stretch, roll over and fall off the counter. What was out of the ordinary about this was that, whereas it is obligatory for all falling cats to achieve a state of feet-firstness while in mid-descent, Rover landed on his back.

This may have been a display of parlour magic; or he may simply have been too lazy to turn before hitting the floor. Personally, I think it was yet another facet of his uncattishness. At any rate, a few weeks later I was the guest speaker at a literary luncheon when the lady of the dinner party came up.

'Hello, how is your cat?' she asked with as much of a smile as a new face-lift would permit. 'Still tripping over himself?'

I laughed indulgently, walked away and took shelter in the lee of the great and good Maeve Binchy. Thumb-screws would not have persuaded me to tell the lady about Rover landing on his back. As the saying goes, it is a poor donkey that trips over the same stone twice.

Certainly, Rover *looked* like a cat. He had a large, square ginger head and amber eyes. There was a riot of freckles around his mouth. Early on, the vet told us that because of a gum infection his teeth were likely to fall out. They did so, except for two incisors of such deadliness that, with a little pressure on his forehead, either one could have functioned as a tin-opener. Because there were no other teeth to get in the way, his small tongue protruded permanently, giving him a village yokel look.

The absence of teeth did not hinder his enjoyment of food. His gums hardened to a degree that put me in mind of a Hollywood chestnut about the making of Cecil B. De Mille's *Samson and Delilah*, in which Victor Mature was called upon to wrestle with a lion. When he demurred, he was assured that the animal was old and toothless.

'So who,' Mr Mature returned, 'wants to be gummed to death?' Rover could have elicited the same reply.

In spite of his slobbish qualities, he was a great epicure. Next door to us was a tall red-bricked building known as the Berwick House Hotel. It was actually a guest house, but an English entrepreneur was determined to upgrade its status, obtain a liquor licence, run it as a gin mill and delight the local residents with a 2 a.m. revving of car engines and slamming of doors. Already, he had opened what styled itself a gourmet

restaurant, which in itself caused the neighbours to declare in the manner of Mr Bennet that they had been delighted quite enough.

Neither Rover – nor Honey for that matter – gave a fig for the pros or the cons of the matter, but Rover did appreciate the excellence of the restaurant. One evening, he brought home an uncooked lemon sole and laid it at our feet with the off-handedness of a Parisian *bon viveur* tipping the hat-check girl at Maxim's. If he could have snapped his paws like fingers, he would have done so. A week later, he strolled in with the less seemly gift of a pheasant's head.

The Berwick House continued to enjoy Rover's patronage until its owner took his pitcher to the well once too often. He had been given permission to extend his kitchen area by thirty square feet; instead, he proceeded to construct a functions room that was ten times as big. The locals protested and the master builder was ordered to desist. Admitting defeat, he emptied the hotel of furnishings, padlocked the doors and returned to England, bitterly complaining that he was a victim of racial prejudice. And of course he was. The Irish are a generous people; they make laws wholly for the English, while they themselves selflessly go without.

I have said that Rover lived for fifteen happy years, apart from a particular nine days. He had enjoyed the best that the Berwick House dustbins could offer. Now and for evermore they were empty, but hope triumphed over experience.

One November evening, like the hotelier before him, he took his pitcher to the well once too often.

The Cat
that Never Was

'I THINK,' my wife said, 'that Rover is gone for good.'

Her logic was unassailable. Switzerland has never produced a chronometer that was as precise as the ebb and flow of Rover's digestive juices. Gastronomy was his passion, and nothing less than death could silence the slam of our cat-door at the very instant that Paule placed his supper dish on the kitchen floor.

During his daily walks, he avoided the main road outside our front door, preferring instead to roam through the back gardens that rose in terraces to Nerano Road. They are Victorian houses in this part of Dalkey, the oldest dating back to the coming of the railway in 1834. Their names – Trafalgar, Jamrud,

Kalafat and Khyber Pass – are paeans to the glories of empire, while the winding roads – Sorrento, Vico and Nerano – remind you that there are Italianate villas in this sheltered corner of Killiney Bay and that the distant Sugar Loaf is our modest Vesuvius.

The back gardens are full of secret places, and unkempt; any cat would swear, paw on heart, that they had been laid out by a feline Capability Brown. Today, however, Rover was elsewhere. He had gone for a stroll and had not come home.

'He's been run over,' Paule said, afraid to go out and see.

I went and looked up and down Coliemore Road, steeling myself for the sight of an inert heap of ginger fur. There was none, and even at a range of two hundred yards the bulk of Rover would hardly be inconspicuous. The only conclusion was that he had for once strayed on to the rocky foreshore in pursuit of water rats, and a wave had carried him off. If he could lose his footing on a stair carpet, there was not much hope for him on a patch of wet seaweed.

Danielle, who had graduated from Trinity, was living and working in New Jersey, and our household now consisted of Paule, her elderly mother and myself. We ate dinner in silence that evening, looking from time to time at Rover's plate, waiting by the kitchen stove. Our ears were cocked for what we knew we would not hear:

the thump and winded gasp of his less than gazelle-like descent from the back yard wall and the clatter of the cat door. It had taken him a month to learn to use it as a means of entry, and another month to realize that it worked both ways.

When I came downstairs next morning and saw that the plate was still untouched, I knew that we had seen the last of him. And yet the more I thought of him having been carried out to sea, the more false the theory rang. Even a tidal wave on the scale of the Severn Bore could not have budged Rover.

Another eight days went by until it was a Sunday evening in November. As in all tales of high drama, nature laid on the special effects, this time in the form of an autumnal gale that sent slates spinning like sycamore pods.

'George, I heard a funny sound today,' the doctor says to his son in Thornton Wilder's *Our Town*. 'It was your mother chopping wood.' The boy, rebuked, weeps for shame. And yet male chauvinism may have its uses. My hearing is not as keen as Paule's, and if I had offered to spare her the task of heaving our rubbish bags down to street-level in readiness for the binmen, I might not have heard what she did: a faint meowing over the roaring of the wind and the sea.

Even when I rushed out of doors in answer to her call, I could make out nothing except the sounds of the storm. 'It was very feeble,' she said. 'I could have sworn. . . . ' Her voice trailed away in disappointment.

If there had been meowing, it did not come again, but she had given me a straw to grasp, and I was not letting go of it. I listened. I went and peered up and down the road and over the sea wall. Nothing. Returning to the house, I looked at the towering black bulk of the deserted Berwick House Hotel. Framed by the darkness of a third-floor window I saw two yellow pinpoints.

Eyes.

An instant later, they had vanished; perhaps they were not eyes at all, but the reflection of a street lamp on the glass pane that shivered in the wind. And yet I knew, because I knew Rover.

'It's him,' I said. 'The fool is trapped in that building.'

There was a private avenue between our house and the hotel, its border lined with heavy stones, and I picked up one of these and prepared to lob it through a ground-floor window.

'We can't,' my law-abiding wife said.

In the moment of hesitation, a thought occurred. What if Rover was not roaming the hotel at large, but confined to a single rooom behind a door that had somehow swung shut behind him? If so, there was not much point in breaking a downstairs window that was still too high to be climbed through. I put the stone

back where it belonged, went into our own house and called the local police station.

The sergeant was most attentive. To my surprise, he did not hem or haw or deliver a sonorous lecture on the law's position as regards forcible entry.

'How long has the animal been incarcerated?' he asked. 'Nine days? Ah wisha, the poor old divil. Then be Jasus, that qualifies as an emergency. Now don't stir. I'll have the fire brigade with yous in no time.'

I hung up. 'He's sending,' I told Paule, 'for the fire brigade.'

She flinched. For people of our parents' generation, the worst disgrace was for a priest or a policeman to be seen coming to the door. Nowadays, if a priest came, it was not to browbeat a drunken master of the house but to solicit a contribution towards a new set of the Stations of the Cross. As for the police, if they appeared at all, it was at our summons. The world had moved on, and between the have-nots and the haves the chasm had narrowed; besides, my likeness was on the walls of at least two pubs: a remarkable achievement for an Irish writer who was not safely dead. But even in the case of people as above reproach as we were, a fire engine might excite speculation. The proverb holds true in the realistic as well as the metaphorical sense that there is no smoke, etc.

I threw her a crumb of comfort. 'They'll never sound

their siren. Not for this.'

I returned to our front steps and, like an utter idiot, called up to the third-floor window: 'Hang on, Rover. It won't be long now.'

The first intimations of rescue appeared ten minutes later when two policemen strolled past. They did not favour us with a glance, I heard one of them speaking into his walkie-talkie. 'Maguire here. We have the premises under surveillance. Over and out.'

I quelled the fear that somehow the message had become garbled and they believed that a gang of armed desperadoes was holed up inside the hotel. By way of defusing this possibility, I bade them a cheery good evening. They were of the old school and each replied in the manner dinned into recruits at the training college at Templemore; which is to say that he nodded darkly. It was the kind of salutation that said: 'This nod is in no way prejudicial to our right to put handcuffs on you tomorrow should we be in the mood.'

The two policemen were no more than an *amuse gueule* for the banquet to come. The entrée arrived in the shape of a police squad car from which four Gardai emerged, unfolding upwards at knee, thigh and waist until it seemed impossible that the car had contained them. In greeting their colleagues who were already *in situ*, one of them remarked that it was a fresh old evening.

'Great drying weather,' the one named Maguire said, and all six fell about like winos.

There followed a lull, broken by chuckles of 'Oh, that's good', repeated at intervals. One gathered that Maguire had reached the end fly-leaf of his joke book.

The six took shelter in our forecourt, giving Paule and myself sidelong looks. I heard us referred to in a whisper as the 'complainants'. Then, from afar, there came a wailing that might have been a dinosaur in its death throes. Our main course was about to be served. Paule looked at me; I saw her lips noiselessly repeat my assurance: 'They'll never sound their siren.'

In contrast to the Gardai, the fire brigade men could not have been jollier. Plainly they had been having a boring evening in the station when news of Rover's plight arrived and turned the night to carnival. They came tumbling off the engine like a troupe of circus acrobats. They all but tossed handkerchiefs to one other and gave glad little cries of 'Allez-oops!' Then they fanned out, attacking the Berwick House from all sides.

What was extraordinary was that we did not actually see them entering the building. Instead, and within a few seconds, they came leaping *out* of it, through doors and windows, like cloned Houdinis. They all but took a bow. I had ever seen such show-offs.

The officer in charge emerged, beaming, through the kitchen door, handed me a flashlight – the electricity had been cut off – and stood to one side. The honour of leading the rescue was clearly to be mine; and so I went pounding up the stairs with the stalwarts of the Dun Laoghaire fire brigade in my wake. I played the light into every room and called: 'Rover?' A puzzled voice behind me said: 'I thought it was a trapped *cat*.'

There was not a stick of furniture in any of the rooms nor a corner in which even a kitten could hide. Within two minutes it was clear that Rover was not in the building. Paule all but burst into tears.

'We were wrong.'

'We weren't. We weren't.' My voice, verging on tantrum, was drumming its heels.

'Then where is he?'

'He . . . he gave us the slip. He's gone home.'

'He can't have.'

'Yes, he has. Go in and see.'

'I tell you he can't have.'

We exchanged a few more has-hasn'ts and can't-haves while the fire brigade looked on sympathetically. Rather than seem a fool, I would swear, black-was-white, that Rover had somehow weaseled past us in the dark. Besides, if we had been mistaken, if he had not been a prisoner for nine days in this Dalkey Chateau d'If, then he was for ever dead, and that was not to be given voice.

Paule went back next-door. The police glowered; the

fire brigade men held their hour. One of them cleared his throat and said: 'Sure anyone can make a—', then thought better of it. We heard our front door slam as Paule returned. It took her a year or so to reach the car park of the Berwick House.

She said: 'He's on his third tin of cat food.'

A great sigh went up; I had never seen so many delighted faces. I thanked the policemen who replied that yerrah, 'twas all in a day's work and went off wearing thin we'll-get-ye-yet smiles. I attempted to press money on the firemen in the name of whatever fund or charity was dear to them. They would have none of it; their little jaunt, they insisted, had enlivened a dull old Sunday. 'It's grand,' the one in charge said, 'to get a stretch of the legs.'

It was only when they had gone, the dinosaur moaning into the distance, that a terrible thought occurred to me. They had not seen a shred of evidence that Rover in fact existed. For all they knew, Paule and I might have been Martha and George mooning over their fantasy son in *Who's Afraid of Virginia Woolf?* To this day, I have wondered if we are talked about in firefighting circles as the couple with the imaginary cat.

There was nothing in the least illusory about the Rover I saw ushering in a new era of prosperity for the makers of Kattomeat. He was by no means emaciated after his ordeal; rather, he had a new svelteness, as if he had just come from a fashionable health farm. Apart from his mental suffering – and 'mental' was not a word that sprang swiftly to the mind in connection with Rover – he seemed in excellent health. During his imprisonment, he had probably obtained water from a dripping tap or a lavatory bowl or licked the condensation from a window pane; what he had found to eat during the nine days did not bear reflection.

The remainder of his life was uneventful. He never again attained his former circumference, but it was a close-run thing. And he more than regained whatever strength he might have lost, as we learned when a length of copper wire became somehow imbedded in his rear end. Our vet, the kindly Mr Rafter, removed it and prescribed antibiotics to counter any infection. Paule winked at me and wrapped one of the pills in a piece of meat, which Rover disposed of in an almighty gulp. Then he hiccuped and spat the pill out.

'Don't worry,' I said masterfully. 'If trickery won't work, brute force will.'

I approached Rover from behind, encircling him with my arms and taking a firm grip on his upper forelegs while Paule dropped the pill into the cavern of his mouth. He turned his head just far enough to favour me with a look of slow contempt. Then, raising a rear paw, he delivered a back-kick that expertly opened the calf of my leg.

He never answered to his name. Some cats come when called, or at least look about them with the incredulity of a monarch who has been whistled at, but I have a theory that either they are responding to a tone of voice or have a name that contains sibilants. Probably, this is why 'Puss' came about: the OED can do no better than say that it was perhaps a name used originally to call a cat. Alas, any attempts I have made to debate this seriously have come to the same fatuous dead end.

'If I was a cat,' I am told, 'and was christened Rover, I'm shagged if *I*'d come when I was called.'

In fact, Rover in time acquired another name, to which he answered if the mood took him. Whenever I stood up to go and pour tea or fetch a magazine, he would usurp my chair the instant my back was turned. Purely as a matter of form, I would groan 'Ah, Jasus'. (So devout are the Irish that they address their Saviour by name several times daily. I had been too long in good company.)

The day came when the conclusion of the Tour de France was shown on television. Our fellow-countryman, Stephen Roche, was the acclaimed winner, and viewers were treated to the spectacle of our Mr Haughey bodily shoving the mayor of Paris to one side in his eagerness to hog the cameras. I gave vent to a disgusted 'Has he no shame?' and added my all-purpose 'Ah, Jasus.'

At this, Rover looked around.

It could have been coincidence, so over the next few days I conducted a series of experiments, done under the most rigorous conditions. The results were unassailable. Rover thought that his name was Ah Jasus.

A Sorbet

(I HAD MEANT to employ *A Digression* as a heading instead of the above affectation, but thought better of it. Especially in a book that is shorter than the average, there is little sense in as good as inviting the reader to skip a chapter and move on to the next cat bit.)

Just as a fondness for one's home can take root and grow, so can its opposite. We lived in 'Theros', as we called it, for six years, and, like many an olde-worlde cottage that is charming on the outside (which our house was not), it ate money. There was storm damage to the roof, flaking paintwork and rotting floorboards. Thanks to us, the local builders, decorators and branch of Rentokil looked upon these as the golden years. Only one tradesman did not go for our financial jugular, and he was the electrician, Mr Shakespeare.

He was a jolly, plump, bald-headed man whose age cannot have been far off eighty, and in the mid-1930s he had introduced the wonder of electric light to my parents' two-room cottage in Kalafat Lane. Now, he was still making Nijinsky-like leaps upon tables and chairs, and for an afternoon's work he demanded £4 and refused to accept an additional penny.

'The name,' he told us, with the smile of a Cheeryble brother, 'is Shakespeare, not Shylock.'

My workroom was next door to the living room and across the hall from the kitchen. Bits of conversation seeped through. Usually, when work is going well, I am immune to all but the most discordant of sounds but on the days when words come slowly or not at all, even the softest whisper will be arraigned as a scape-goat for the empty page.

It was not a writer's house (although I could not tell you what is), but so impatient were we to quit Killiney for Dalkey that we might have been soul-mates of the girl who in her eagerness to marry forgets to take a good look at the bridegroom. As in her case, having made our bed, we had no choice but to lie in it.

One day, Paule saw a sea-front apartment advertised for sale in the *Irish Times*. The exact location was coyly withheld, but in our town such properties had become as rare as hens' teeth. Out of what was no more than purposeless curiosity she called the estate agents, and we were shown the apartment.

It was a duplex; it had five balconies. Dalkey and Killiney hills were to the south; seaward, the views began with James Joyce's tower, four-hundred yards away, then embraced the mile-long granite piers of Dun Laoghaire harbour. Beyond, the Liffey stretched its arms towards the Hill of Howth across the bay. The sea was no more than a few feet from the windows: a granite outcrop and an acre of grass combined to be a cats' paradise. The price was as stupendous as the view.

In twenty-nine years of marriage, I had never known Paule to ask outright for anything – true artistry, of course, lies in *not* asking – but within a minute of entering the apartment she said: 'I wouldn't mind having this.'

For her, not to mind having something is the ultimate manifestation of heart's desire. As for myself, the more I saw of the place, the more I would not have minded having the upstairs workroom. I asked my accountant if the place was within our reach.

His name was Russell Murphy. He was tall, looming and saturnine; his nickname was 'The Monk'. He had no capacity for leisure; once, on holiday, he had been observed sitting on the shingle beach at Skerries wearing a necktie, charcoal black jacket and striped trousers.

He was a man of countless kindnesses; when a colleague fell mortally ill, Russell accompanied him to Lourdes. He was stage-struck; he sent flowers to actresses on first nights; theatre people who were in trouble with the inland revenue went to him for help and received derisory bills for his services. In the age of the 'cute whoor', few professional men were more respected. To his juniors, he was Godlike: a leviathan among minnows. He approved of my loathing of the Provos and, at his own suggestion, had become my investment broker as well as accountant.

On the rare occasions when I called to his office, he would stride about, his fingers interlaced behind his head, and intone his credo: 'Bricks and mortar, bricks and mortar!' Of late, he had been on my conscience; I had found myself – and I had no idea why – sneaking my earnings into a bank account, rather than entrusting them to him for investment. I felt disloyal. When I asked him about the apartment, he hemmed for a bit, declared the price to be exorbitant, and – as ever, a realist – knew that I was set on the place.

'But *of course* you can afford it!' he boomed.

I agreed to pay what was asked, and at once the vendor, recognizing a pigeon when he saw one, turned the screw for another £10,000. His solicitor's letter came as I was leaving for London on a business trip. I promised my wife that I would call Russell from the airport.

'Paule is afraid you'll advise us against the apartment,' I told him. 'I know we're being conned, but her heart is set on it.' So, in a way, was mine.

'Leave it to me,' Russell said. 'Off you go to London, and blessings be upon you.'

It was the last time I heard his voice.

After I had spoken with him, he called Paule to assure her that all was well. His final words to her were: 'You do trust me, don't you?'

Few people knew that he was ill with cancer of the lung. A doctor had given him six months to live (why, I wonder, is it always six, never five or seven?), and within three weeks of our conversation I was writing his obituary for the *Irish Times*. Being ever too lazy to compile a scrapbook, I must rely on memory, and my impression is that I laid emphasis on his sense of honour. Honour was, I think I said, Russell's byword.

The irony is delectable, for not long afterwards one of his junior partners called to our house. He sat, nervously, in an armchair. Beside me on the sofa, Rover lay on his back. He was the picture of inelegance, tongue protruding as usual, legs wide apart, his white underbelly facing the ceiling. Before I had poured a drink for my visitor, I knew what he had to say, and it was as brief as it was simple. The late Russell Murphy was an embezzler.

There were other victims besides myself, including

his closest friend, to one of whose daughters he had been godfather, but I was the star turn. I had seen the last of nearly a quarter of a million pounds. My caller kept telling me how much was gone, whereas I kept begging to know how much was left.

It could have been worse. There was, for instance, my 'signature', witnessed by Russell and appended to a loan application for yet another quarter of a million, but he had managed to repay the last of that shortly before he died. And in one respect he had held true; by now the new apartment was irrevocably ours.

When my visitor had gone, I went up to our local. It was a Tuesday, the day that Paule meets her friends for lunch and a drink, and even before I pushed the door open there came the unique and yet not uncommon sound of six women all talking at the same time – to this day I have no idea if they simultaneously listen to each other as well, or if it matters not in the least. I took Paule to one side and told her my news. She loves a joke, the dirtier the better, and composed herself to laugh at the punch-line.

It took half a minute for her to realize that there was none. She rallied and said: 'If it's true, why are you smiling?'

I had not the faintest idea, then or for a long time afterwards. As much to my surprise as anyone's, the smile refused to go away, so I tried to explain it with

cod philosophy. I shamelessly fobbed off condolences
with: 'As my wise old mother would have said, "Wasn't
it great, son, that you had so much money to lose!" "

(The truth was that my wise old mother would have
cursed Russell Murphy, together with his seed, breed
and generation, and then castigated me as a gobshite
for ever having trusted him.)

Only slowly did I come to realize the reason for the
smile. For once in my life, I had found out something
about myself that was not dislikeable, and it was that
I did not really care about the money.

When the bubble burst, the press had a field day. No
one ever discovered what Russell had done with his
plunder; the theories included wildcat property invest-
ments, an expensive mistress and riotous living. As for
the last of these, it was true that whenever he sent me
a postcard, it arrived by chauffeured limousine. And
certainly, I would hate to have paid for all those first-
night flowers. Contrary to legend, not every Irish
actress is another Bernhardt.

The experience did carry a sting in its tail, and in an
unexpected way. *Today Tonight* is an RTE current affairs
programme, and the Russell Murphy bombshell was
the very stuff of television. I appeared on camera for
some minutes, but it was not a success; my disincli-
nation to rail against the fates in general and Russell
Murphy in particular was not to my interviewer's

liking. She became peevish; my refusal to whinge was admirable, but I had taken it too far; the viewers were entitled to see a drop or two of blood.

Her final question was: 'Do you have a good conscience about the money that was stolen?'

I made a light reply of some kind. It is said that often when a man receives a stab wound, the pain does not come until later, and it was only when I was driving away from the studio that the thrust went home.

It came to me that in Ireland of the Begrudgeries, I was not much better thought of than Russell, for whom to this day I still harbour a furtive affection. The stolen money had been hard-earned over twenty-five years, but that, so the interviewer was implying, in no way excused my indecency in possessing it.

(In a brazen moment, I was tempted to give these few pages a wholly spurious relevance by pleading that there exist human cats as well as the other kind. Better not; the biscuit-coloured Burmese that sits on my lap as I type would deeply resent the slur.)

The Walk-Ons

A WALK-ON is the theatrical equivalent of a film extra. He is one of a crowd; he carries a spear or wears a cloth cap; he makes a few noises, either exultant or execratory, and is soon gone. During Rover's lifetime, there were three walk-on cats that entered downstage left, muttered 'Rhubarb, rhubarb' and strolled off again, and he managed to outlive two of them. This was surprising, for his accident-proneness did not diminish with age.

To reach our apartment, one must ascend three flights of stairs, each doubling back on the next. The steps are of rough-cast concrete, with a green woollen stair carpet that does not quite extend to the edge. It always bothered me that our cats when going up or down disdained to negotiate the half-landings; when they were a stair or two short of one, they would take a short cut by hopping across the void.

I suffer from vertigo. In my youth, I actually ran down the spiral staircase of the Eiffel Tower; today, I doubt if I could bring myself to use the elevator. The palms of my hands grow damp at the memory of looking upon Thessaly's plains from the rock pillars of Meteora, and I all but swoon when reliving the bus ride from Capri to Anacapri. But for stomach-grinding nausea, there was nothing to equal the sight of Rover going down the stairs of our apartment block.

A few months before he died, it occurred to him that he had business to transact in the shrubbery that borders our car park. I was going out of doors at the time, so, mumbling to himself, he preceded me. As usual, I averted my eyes for a moment as he made a rheumatic hop across the gap between the flights. This time, however, he froze midway with his hindlegs one step up from the landing and his forepaws one step down. It was as if he had all of a sudden forgotten where he was going and why.

'Ah Jasus, make up your mind,' I groaned.

It was the wrong thing to say, for it caused Rover to decide that his business, whatever it was, could not have been all that important. He embarked upon a U-turn. Naturally, he tripped.

His sixteen pounds hung over the abyss like a carcase on a butcher's hook, while his forepaws scrabbled desperately for a hold on the rough concrete of the upper step. I had a vision of him plummeting to the basement, with nothing to break his free fall but the zig-zag of the narrow iron banisters.

It was all over in a few seconds, but for me time took on a meaning that would have sent Albert Einstein hotfooting it back to his blackboard. While I stood, paralysed by terror, Rover took a year or so to raise one of his rear paws until he at last gained an extra purchase on the upper step and heaved his weight to safety. It was like watching Harold Lloyd in *Safety Last*.

Unruffled, he then ambled upstairs, taking the uppermost step with his usual leaden bounce. This was accompanied by a guttural request that I open our door for him. As he strolled in, I heard him call out to Paule that he was home again and that she need not feel inhibited from advancing the dinner hour. For myself, I had intended to take my letters to the post; instead, it was as much as I could do to drive as far as the pub.

During that last year, we could see that he was slowing down. When autumn came, Paule and I took a sea cruise around Indonesia, and in the ship's boutique there was a lifelike toy cat for sale. It was big, fat and marmalade: the image, in fact, of Rover. Its eyes were closed, and its mouth was set in an expression of extreme displeasure. It cost seventy-five dollars.

When we were a few days at sea, I put three US 25-cent pieces into one of the poker machines in the tiny casino. A royal flush came up, earning me three hundred dollars, and I celebrated by buying the cat. We called it Mog.

Seeing him scowling from the pillow when we retired to our stateroom, it was impossible not to believe that Rover was afloat with us, and on the journey home, I caused a mild sensation at airports along the way by allowing Mog's orange tail to protrude from my travel bag.

'Would you like to see a fat cat?' I coyly asked the customs officer at Dublin Airport.

'Only if it's dead,' he said.

The joke, small as it was, fell flat. I could not shake off the presentiment that Rover would soon go the way of Prissy, Tinkle and Honey. Between Paule and myself, there lurked the unspoken accord that Mog's role would be to fill his space. Not even a live cat could take his place.

Rover did die a couple of months later, and I was reminded of the moment in *The Quiet Man*, when a thwarted Victor McLaglen says of his rival, John Wayne: 'He'll regret this to his dying day, if he lives that long.'

If I may employ a not dissimilar Irish bull to pay tribute to an Irish cat, then, given Rover's talent for disaster, it was a near-miracle that he lived until the day he died. Meanwhile, the sight of his effigy sitting, paws folded, on a stool in our living room, has caused many an unwary visitor to emit a most gratifying shriek.

The most remarkable of our three 'walk-ons' was not our cat at all. A stray, he had been found wandering in Cork and so was given the name of Corker. It suited him, for he was the most self-possessed cat I have known. Indeed, I first laid eyes on him sitting on a barstool. That is not clumsy syntax. I mean that Corker was on a barstool next but one to mine. He wore a collar, and attached to it was a dangling lead. He was immersed in a contemplation of the row of beer pumps. It would not have surprised me if he had produced an *Evening Herald* and started doing the crossword.

His straight man (again, I cannot perpetrate the solecism of 'owner') recognized me by sight, thereby honouring the adage that more people know Tom-fool than Tom-fool knows. His name was Michael Andrews, and his business was the selling of out-of-the-way books. He was a bachelor and a loner; apart from an aged mother who lived in Devon, Corker was his only kin, and perhaps kith as well. Michael had no sooner introduced himself then he paid his dues with a long

and ripely funny anecdote about an aeroplane trip across the Mediterranean ('Turn left for Malta, right for Gib'). Meanwhile, Corker deigned to refresh himself from an ashtray filled with water. People came to stare; he ignored them; his sang-froid was awesome. At closing time, I was allowed to peer into Michael's car: on the rear seat there was a litter tray, food and drink, and a cat basket, blanketed and snug. Apart from there being no tablet of mint chocolate on the pillow, it was the ideal home from home.

Corker was a one-off; the kind of prodigy that makes one sick if he happens to belong to someone else. Early each evening, Michael would drive him to Sorrento Point, where the bays of Dublin and Killiney meet. There, as the cat vanished into the tanglewood of an untamed parkland, his straight man went home for dinner or to pay business calls. Two or three hours later, Michael would return and call Corker by name, and without fail a small grey ghost would drop down from a branch.

If, in the course of his overnight travels, Michael encountered a toffee-nosed hotelier who declared cats to be *non grata* in his establishment, Corker would be sternly commanded to spend the night in the car. All cats know when a voice has a wink and a nudge in it, and so he would instead make for the shrubbery and wait. As soon as Basil Fawlty had retired for the night, a voice would whisper from an open first-floor window, and with one leap the outcast was over the sill and enjoying the much-touted h. and c., c.h., Scand. duv. and int. sprung matt.

Michael's total devotion to Corker was touching and, for me, a little worrying. My own affections run so deep that out of a sense of self-preservation, I like to have an extra cat in hand for a rainy day. And the rain could not have come down more heavily when at last the unthinkable happened and Corker went missing.

It is easy to find a lost cat here in our town, where it could not walk the length of Castle Street without being asked its name, what it had for dinner, and wasn't the Dalkey Players' latest a howl. But Corker had disappeared in one of the immense suburbs of south London, where every redbricked house is a clone of the next, and people do not look at each other, never mind at cats. Michael was distraught. For days he tramped about, peering into pocket-handkerchief gardens; he wrote out a hundred 'Lost' notices and pinned them to trees.

As I told him afterwards, he should have had more faith in his friend's genius. When all hope was gone, there came a ring and a meow at the door, and Corker walked in, followed by a uniformed member of London's finest. That prodigy among cats had probably grown tired of sitting in a tree, waiting to be found. At any rate, he finally took the remedy into his own paws, walked into the nearest police station and gave himself up.

Two years ago, I had a call from Michael. He was heart-broken. Corker was dying. There was nothing I could do except make sympathetic noises. When I next saw the familiar car in the town, there was no cat basket on the rear seat; instead, a small, meek dog peered out at me. As in the case of our Rover's lookalike, Mog, he was there to fill another's space without taking his place.

Again, I congratulated myself on avoiding the folly of ever having only one cat. Such smugness does not go unpunished for long, as I was to find out.

* * *

Our second walk-on cat was Oscar. He resembled Sylvester of the Warner Brothers cartoons, who was forever thwarted in his pursuit of Tweetie-Pie. Oscar, however, would have given the canary short shrift.

He was one of a job lot of eight, whose custodians were, for want of their real names, Joe and Peg Phelan. Joe was the kind of man whose train is always pulling out of the station when he arrives. He was easy-going, an obliger of others whose fate seemed to be to do a charge hand's work for a labourer's pay. Peg was a sentimental soul; she doted on old songs, old times, old ways. She had great brown eyes that forever threatened to fill with tears; like Ben Bolt's sweet Alice, she trembled with fear at a frown. She was as tough as old boots.

She had a vocation for grandeur. Much as a dipsomaniac craves whisky, so she hungered for the fat of the land. In her late forties, she rebelled; she was tired of feeding on life's scrag-end. She was, she told herself, a woman with as natural a talent for gracious living as Pavarotti had for singing 'Galway Bay'.

Well, Ireland had let her down, and now the devil's cure to it. Henceforth, it could fend for itself; she and Joe would go to Texas, where her sister lived and only fools and utter gobshites were not as rich as God. At her bidding, the family sold up and set off for the New World. They would be back, she told us gaily, within five years and buy not only a house that would have all Dalkey's eyes out on sticks, but a cabin cruiser on the Shannon. They would take us on it for weekends, and meanwhile would we look after Oscar? Yes, you will, Peg's brimming eyes said, sure you can't refuse me. Hers was a whim of granite.

They had already disposed of Oscar's seven siblings, and he had never been the pick of the bunch. He was twelve; he lived mainly out of doors, and in consequence the optional extra of house-training had been foregone.

I did not much love Oscar.

There are those who allege that to keep a pet denotes an inadequacy. People who do so have a need, we are told, to be admired, to be depended on, to subject an animal to the power they do not possess over their fellow humans. They want an adoration that is total and uncritical. For myself, I like cats for their beauty, their good company, their grace and their coquetry. In my life, only one has ever fawned on me; that was Dubh (pronounced *dove*), and I confess that I was human enough to fawn back.

Oscar reminded me of a plump waiter named Tony in Giovanni's restaurant off St Martin's Lane, who one day said to me quite out of the blue: 'I want you to know, sir, that you don't impress me.' Clearly, I did not impress Oscar, either. Come the revolution, his look kept saying, mine would be the first head in the basket. Now and again, and so far unlike Tony in Giovanni's, he bit me.

The American humorist, Will Rogers, frequently said: 'I never met a man I didn't like.' If this is true, then besides lacking good taste, he missed a great deal of fun. To swathe all humankind in the same coarse blanket of affection is to the sensible mind not only undiscriminating, but downright promiscuous. Cats deserve the occasional honour of being disliked, especially since the more doting of their custodians like to think they are paying their Sheba or Jason a compliment with the accolade of 'nearly human'.

Oscar's twilight days were peaceful, and he scowled at me for a full two years before the day when he peed on his last Wilton. Meanwhile, his previous landlords, Joe and Peg, have still not come back from San Antonio, except on visits. Their lives are not quite barren; on Sundays, they can at least go and look at the Alamo.

* * *

Gatsby, our third walk-on, was an elegant red-point Siamese, who, instead of coming properly on-stage, hovered in the wings. He resembled half of a pair of tall onyx bookends. He was to be my birthday present from our friend, Joan Lohan.

When it comes to gifts, Joan's habit is to buy first and ask questions later, and on my behalf Paule's reaction was a flat thank-you-but-no-thank you. I felt like a ventriloquist's dummy, but I could see her point. What with Dubh, the incontinent Oscar, and Rover gumming cat-food by the mountain and walking into doors, our cup was already full to overflowing.

And so Joan kept Gatsby, as she called him, for herself, and today her menagerie consists of him, a Siamese named Chang, a Burmese named Ming (*our* present to *her*), a venerable and testy poodle named Coco and a shrill strawberry blonde mongrel named

Trixie. The only irregularity is that no one has troubled to explain to Gatsby that he was not and is not my cat.

He knows better. The first time I laid eyes on him, he at once stepped on to my lap and sat there, unbudgeable. He has been doing so for nine years now. He does not flirt or invite intimacy; he is simply performing a rite of ownership – his ownership of me, that is.

Man-upping, one could call it.

* * *

And so, to Dubh.

Dubh

'I FOUND him straying on the road,' the girl said, 'poor little thing, he was certain to get run over.'

The kitten was perhaps six inches from nose to base of tail. His eyes were yellow, or they soon would be; and he was jet black except for a white blaze on his breast. Oddly, his nose was not concave; it curved forward in a mildly Roman fashion, as if to suggest that at least one of his forebears had had connections within the Quality.

The girl was a stranger to us. We were living then in the house that looked across to Dalkey Island, and stirring times as yet lay ahead; Rover, for instance, was still to serve his nine days' porridge in the deserted building next door. Our caller had perhaps espied a light behind our living-room curtains.

The kitten's chances of survival on Coliemore Road after nightfall were certainly small. The girl told us that she thought she knew which local family he belonged to, but she disliked bothering people so late in the evening. (We, apparently, were the botherable kind.) She did not dare take him home with her – either she had other cats or an unfriendly dog; I forget which.

'I thought,' she said, 'that you might keep him . . . just for the one night.'

She held him towards us in her cupped hands. It made him look even tinier and more pitiable than he was.

When I closed the front door behind her and returned to our kitchen-cum-day room, Paule was looking doubtfully at the kitten.

'I wonder if she will,' she said.

'What?'

'Come back tomorrow.'

'She said she would.'

'She'd better. If she doesn't, we'll be stuck with him.'

This was the signal for the newcomer to launch into his audition. His heart was set on stardom. Rover had come into the room, and, as he looked on in stupefaction, the kitten cavorted, leaped and rolled over; he purred, head-butted us and chased his tail. We ached to tell him 'Stop, the part is yours!', but he was taking no chances. He ran up one of my arms and down the other. On the velveteen tablecloth, he was a dervish; he fandango-ed, pirouetted and ended up with a feline buck-and-wing so rumbunctious that one could almost see his vaudevillian's derby hat, kid gloves and cane.

When he had finished, he ate. His mouth did not look at all big until it went into action, and then it earned him the immediate nickname of the Mechanical Digger. Replete, he lay on his back, his black stomach globular, and went to sleep, smiling. He resembled the kitten, Figaro, in the Disney *Fantasia*.

'Oh, God,' Paule moaned, 'don't tell me that that woman is going to come back and take him from us.'

She was so distraught that I did a hoarse Brando mumble and said: 'I'll make her an offer she can't refuse.'

Paule was not convinced. All next day, she was tense, waiting for the sound of the doorbell. It did not come, then or the day after, and slowly and joyfully it dawned on us that we had been hoaxed. Probably the girl had disposed of an entire litter by the same ploy.

We called the kitten Dubh, and he grew into a lithe young cat with a genius for culling the local bird and rodent population. Once, there was a great commotion at the cat door, and a moment later our Nimrod appeared lugging a newly-deceased magpie. With

Rover, I have seen seagulls perch and strut on the balcony outside my workroom window, all but daring him to leap at them and go plunging to the rocks below; they were too wary to play such games with Dubh.

He took not much pity on my vertigo. One day, I heard my wife scream and, on rushing into an upstairs bedroom, saw that he was outside on the narrow window ledge, looking in. There was no knowing how he had got there unless he had flown; and, as for our opening the window and hauling him in, a master carpenter of a bygone age had made it burglar-proof with a row of six-inch nails. I ran down to the yard below, looked up, tried not to faint, and implored Dubh to stay perfectly still. The man who mended our roof had left a long two-by-four behind him by way of a keepsake, and it occurred to me that if I could raise it to the level of the window-sill, it might serve as, literally, a kind of catwalk.

I hoisted it to the perpendicular and tottered about for a bit, like a drunken Scotsman with a caber. Dubh looked on with interest, then, as I tore down my wife's washing line, it occurred to him that, while fun was fun, the rampaging plank – which was now waving my clean Y-fronts about like the flag of an obscure banana republic – was only inches from his nose. He jumped, not onto the plank, but clear of it.

It was a magnificent leap, worthy of a lemur. He

landed, unerringly, on top of a wooden trellis that could not have been more than an inch and a half wide. I reached up, lifted him down and cursed him. As I made to go indoors, there was a faint noise from behind me. I turned and looked. He was back on the window sill.

Our move to the apartment overlooking the sea was only grist to his mill. On fine days, as I worked, he would sit outside, performing his ablutions on the stone balustrade of a balcony. I tried not to look. Then, if the fancy took him, he would disappear upwards, and I knew that he was on the roof itself, which was steep and slated.

It made my head swim to think of him overhead, sitting on a chimney-pot, perhaps, and looking down on the parked cars and the neighbours' groundling cats. And he never returned the way he had gone; instead, having climbed the north face, he would descend to the balcony that was on the far side of my workroom. I had a vision of him losing his footing on the slates and of a ball of black fur hurtling silently past my window.

He never fell. Instead, there would be a small breathless thump as he came to land on the tiles of the balcony. He then peered in at me to ensure that I had thrilled to every moment of his feat.

Cats, I know beyond all doubt, have extra-sensory perception. Two days before we go on holiday, ours become tense and disconsolate; they haunt the bed-room for a sight of a suitcase, and when it appears they sit in it, defying us to pack. A non-romantic – than whom no more miserable specimen exists – would argue that their antennae had picked up the tensions caused by our pre-travel nerves. One cannot, however, so easily account for Dubh's behaviour when Paule's mother died.

She had turned eighty. She occupied a bedsitter on the upper floor of the duplex, across the landing from my workroom. Dubh became 'her' cat, either from pref-erence or to put space between himself and Rover, who would speed him on his various errands with a swipe from an orange paw. At any rate, when he was not foraging out of doors or sunning himself on the roof, he would sit quietly in her lap.

She became ill with shingles. In itself, it was not a fatal illness, but over three years the constant pain sapped her strength. She lost weight and became increasingly enfeebled. On a November evening at about seven, Dubh gave the soft quacking sound that signified his wish to be let out. His pastimes were simple; he liked to sit in the shrubbery, sniff the fra-grances, go to the bathroom, bury the consequences and, in general, ensure that all was well with the world.

It was a Monday, the evening on which I usually met a friend for a drink at our local. The pattern was that, returning at eleven, my car's headlamps would pick up two smaller yellow lights in a dark corner of the apartment block. A familiar soft 'wah' would greet me, and Dubh would emerge from the shadows to lead the way upstairs, rubbing himself languorously against the iron uprights of the banisters. On this evening, he had been absent and about his affairs for two hours when I started to leave for the pub. I heard Paule cry out from upstairs, where she had discovered her mother to be either dead or near death.

I telephoned for the doctor and an ambulance. The former confirmed that the old lady had quitted her body; the latter took away what remained. It was all over with bewildering swiftness. Although the end had not been unexpected, it was sudden, and, rather than sit staring at one another, we got in touch with friends, who came at once. After a hour or so, I thought of Dubh and went downstairs. I clapped my hands, peered into the dark and, after a minute, detected a movement, black against black.

There were perhaps eight people in our living room. Voices were muted, balancing bromides of cheer with an innate regard for the decencies; for delicacy, the Irish, so often graceless in their pleasures, have no equals at times of mourning. To my surprise, Dubh walked straight into the room and sat under a chair. Usually, he was shy of visitors, always retreating upstairs to the bedsitter, which in any case was his eyrie. This evening, when our guests left, he refused to budge.

Down the years, Rover's bed had been ours, his dead weight creating a deep valley in the bedclothes. In the small hours, Paule or I would awake, coverless and freezing, and tug at the duvet in an attempt to retrieve a small share of it. This caused the slumbering Rover to levitate slowly. Then, as soon as sleep returned and one's grip loosened, he sank again, taking the duvet with him. On this particular night, while trying to position my legs on one side of him or the other, I felt a tugging at my hair. Dubh had settled for the night on my pillow and was lying on it. Thereafter, it was his bed, too.

There was no possible way in which he could have known of the events of the evening, and yet he did know. When he came indoors, not only was he aware that his friend was gone, but he knew the how of her going, for it was a full year before he would go upstairs, and as long again before he could be cajoled to enter the bedsitter.

Dubh did not stay bereaved for long; he became 'my' cat, just as he had been hers. We cemented what the French would call our *amitié amoureuse* shortly after Paule and I returned from holiday to discover that he had been in the wars. Two serpents had come into his

Eden in the shape of a pair of young Burmese cats who were to be our new neighbours. To humans who paused to admire their sleek handsomeness, they were the brothers Jekyll; they purred, preened and nuzzled most disgustingly; with other cats, they were Edward Hydes of the deepest dye. Even though they were parvenus, they plainly saw Dubh as a rival hoodlum muscling in on their territory. He was no longer the lithe, young slayer of magpies, and they gave him a going over so savage that for a week one could not see him without shuddering.

His good looks soon returned, and to our delight his assailants moved to a new address, but he was not his old self. His flanks went hollow, his coat became dull and he began to pull his fur out by the mouthful. Our vet, Colm Rafter, could discover no physical cause and suggested that I make an appointment with a specialist at the veterinary clinic in Ballsbridge. There, a specimen of tissue was taken and examined; meanwhile Dubh stood on the metal examination table, shaking with fear. I stroked him, then saw him put his head inside my jacket.

It was a gesture of trust so total that at that moment I was for ever lost.

The specialist was talking to me. 'Has a new cat come into your neighbourhood?'

'Two,' I said. 'Although they've already moved

away.'

'That's it, then,' he said. 'This fellow is having a nervous breakdown.'

While he was writing out a prescription for sedatives, I put the open cat basket on the table. It had taken Paule and me all of five minutes to force Dubh into it; struggling in grim silence, he had seemed to possess three heads and an infinity of limbs. Now, recognizing his road home, he not only hopped into the basket of his own accord but actually ducked his head so that I might the more easily close the lid.

He recovered. He grew plump again and sleek. Meanwhile, our friendship flourished. One of his traits, at once endearing and unnerving, was to climb on my lap, push his nose against mine, cry softly and, from a few inches away, regard me solemnly without a blink of his yellow eyes.

His gaze became so intense and so urgent that once, when no one was listening, I heard myself ask: 'Is there a human soul inside you?'

There was a soft, answering 'Wah'.

About a year ago, as I write, Rover died and I found myself in the trap into which others had fallen and of which I had so complacently steered clear. For the first time, I did not have a cat in hand for that rainy day.

If there were misgivings, I brushed them aside. A small befurred creature should not, after all, be at the centre of any sane man's life, certainly not mine. I had my family, friends, and a cherished enemy or two. I had my work – this book was to be the next in line. There were the perks: good food, talk, old films, and Provence in summer. There was the joy of living in a town that was loonier than Dylan Thomas's Llaregyb (only the other day, a man hailed me in our local, then excused himself, saying that he thought I was someone else. He added, no less apologetically: 'I wouldn't like you to think I was being friendly.')

Besides, if an accident-prone, grossly over-weight cat such as Rover could live to be fifteen, then Dubh, at twelve, was still in his prime. No, best forget it. Sufficient unto the day and all that.

We are not day people; for us, midnight is the shank of the evening. In the living room at one a.m., six months after the last of Rover, I heard Dubh emit a terrible cry. He gave two or three convulsive kicks and then stared at me. It was a while before I realized he was dead.

I had never felt so alone; for me, it was as if a child had died. That is probably a monstrous thing to say, and I am quite sure that it betokens a defect in my nature. There are two people inside every writer: the layman, and the anatomist who dissects and arraigns him. In my own case, the second man could only wonder at the quantity of tears that were shed and the refusal of the wound to heal.

For a time, I have suspected that my daughter, who now works and lives in London, is so vulnerable to the pain of loss that she protects herself behind a palisade of distance. If this is so, it perhaps comes from me. With parents, their age and frailty alert you to what is to come, but in Dubh's case I had neglected to put on armour. The detached anatomist told me, and might have saved his breath, to stop the moping; it was, after all, only a cat. When our next-door neighbour mentioned Dubh by name in front of me, I saw Paule give her a look that was a danger signal: *Don't start him off*.

For years, whenever we went away from home, we employed a lady to live in and take care of the apartment and the cats. My first attempt to find such a paragon had been an advertisement in the *Irish Times* personals headed 'Cat Sitter Wanted'. This evoked an unsigned reply from a County Limerick reader who told us in some detail what she proposed to do to the cats, if entrusted with them. Her letter ended: 'Yous ****ing heathens, you.' (The asterisks are, for the third time, mine.) In the end, a treasure in the persona of one Mary Watson came to us from Cork. Now, with Dubh gone, Paule and I played the roles of Job and his comforters by telling ourselves that henceforth going away would involve no more than locking the front door behind us.

Life was suddenly simple and desirable. So we told each other, if not ourselves. On one thing we were agreed and immovable. We had done with cats. The Liffey might run dry and the Hill of Howth crumble; prelates might know love and politicians become honest.

Never, not ever again.

Something Else

OUR APARTMENT seemed every day to become emptier. When I ventured to mention it to my other self, the anatomist, he replied sneeringly that I was a man of straw, that my resolve was faltering. I retorted that he had his hash and parsley. Could not a person merely remark of a room that it no longer had echoes? Good heavens, I chortled hollowly, was he so advanced in dotage as to suggest that I would invite the same heartbreak twice?

I remembered all the illnesses and hurts, the battles lost or Pyrrhically won. I relived the visits to the vet. I recalled the winter nights when the alarm clock in my brain went off to remind me that Dubh had not yet come in, wherepon I would go downstairs and peer out, shivering, into the near-dawn, my feet bare on a wet flagstone. I thought again of how he played Edward Whymper on our roof while my nerves turned to wet muesli.

Now we were free. No longer would we fret over a small, animated, bundle of fur that died too soon. The litter tray and the food and water bowls had been spirited away. The marmalade Mog, with a woollen heart, sat for ever silent on his stool in the living room, and he was enough for us. To use the title of a Wodehouse story, it was goodbye to all cats.

I set myself to begin work on this book. The w.p. blinked on, and I punched up the text name for the first page, *Rover 1*, but inside my head I heard a plaintive and well-familiar 'wah', and it was impossible to write for tears. I was like the love-crossed soprano in a '30s film, who kept breaking down in the middle of her great aria. Perhaps I should abandon the book and write another stage play.

I don't know how I first came to suspect that Paule and her friend, Joan, had been cruising the locality, inspecting catteries.

'You're going to lumber me with a kitten,' I said, accusingly.

'No,' my wife replied, with such absolute candour that my heart at once sank. 'We're only looking at catteries.'

'No harm in that,' Joan said.

It was as if two men coming out of a gunsmith's shop had sworn on their mothers' graves that they were pacifists. I implored Paule not to confront me with a whiskered and purring *fait accompli*. She gave me her sacred word of honour; there would be no kitten. That should have been direct enough for any man. I thanked her and went up to my workroom feeling like a mother who has just attended a lecture from King Herod on the subject of child-care.

By coincidence, a letter came a few days later. It was from the lady whose two Burmese cats had temporarily ruined Dubh's good looks. She had read in my *Sunday Independent* column that he was gone, and wanted to commiserate. She herself had moved house to a cul-de-sac close to a main road, and passing cars had soon done for both her terrors.

An idea formed. I was not unlike the man who, when sentenced to hang, determines that at least he will go out in his own fashion. If a kitten was inevitable – and, if I were honest, the anatomist in me spoke truth and I was weakening – it would be a Burmese. A local pet shop provided me with the names of breeders.

The first number I called did not answer; the second was that of Carmel Madden in Ratoath, County Meath. When I told her that I wanted to buy a Burmese kitten, she narrowly avoided saying: 'Oh, you do, do you?' Instead, she merely asked me twenty or so questions. Who was our vet? Where did he live? Had we had cats previously? Why did I want a Burmese? That last was the toughest question. She might just as well have asked why I wanted a cat, full stop, in which event I could only have lamely replied: for company. That Sunday, Paule, Joan and I drove the thirty miles to Ratoath.

I have few natural talents, but one of them is the great gift of serendipity. A few years ago, cruising eastwards out of the Canal du Midi, we arrived by wild accident at Frontignan on the very evening of the canal's tricentennial celebrations. As we sat on deck drinking the local muscat while fireworks exploded overhead, one of our lady crew-members said: 'This sort of thing keeps happening to you, doesn't it?' And yes, it does, and it did that Sunday in Ratoath.

Carmel proved to be a warm lady whose persona was comprised of a vast, built-in hug. There is a Dublin phrase for being totally at ease and in the kind of company where all may be said and all is understood. Achieve such a state and you are 'in your grannie's', and, once Carmel was satisfied that to us an exotic kitten was not simply this month's fad, our grannie's was precisely where we were.

Not only did she breed Burmese kittens, but Balinese

as well, and there was a litter of each, born a day apart six weeks previously. A dozen of them crawled over our feet, behind cushions and under chairs. At teatime, they surrounded the same vast plate of tuna; the Burmese tails sticking up, thin and spiked, those of the Balinese curving in a promise of lushness to come. I looked at Paule.

It was I-wouldn't-mind time again. She said: 'I wouldn't mind having two. That one and that.'

She might have been choosing a Danish pastry and an eclair at a *patisserie* counter. Both kittens were male; a biscuit-coloured Burmese and a shy, ivory Balinese. Throwing sanity to the winds, I also bought a gleaming dark Burmese as an early Christmas present for Joan, who had visibly started to drool. When, seven weeks later, our purchases were of an age to be taken home, she called him Ming and was dismayed to learn that the intergalactic villain of the old Flash Gordon serials was known as Ming the Merciless. Actually and given the kitten's genius for depredation, she had named him aptly.

Our two lived up to their names as well. The Burmese became The Pooka, which means a mischievous Irish spirit. Like all his breed, he had a square, open Cagney-ish face and was unneurotic, fearless, riotously affectionate, incorrigible, and brawling and angelic by turns. Also, there was plainly critic's blood in him, for he had not been in his new home five minutes before he was in my workroom and upon the desk with one paw firmly planted on the 'erase' key of my w.p.

Around his neck there were folds of loose flesh in such lavish quantities that one would have thought he could have accommodated another kitten besides himself. With all that spare skin, it should have been easy to take hold of him, but on his first morning with us, when I went downstairs for the letters, he shot past me and rolled about on the top landing, inches from the edge. I felt my vertigo come back like the twinge of an old war-wound.

The keyword for the Balinese was, and still is, 'cautious'. He resembled a long-coated Siamese. His ears, gloves and socks were a deep brown; his coat was a silken yellowish-white ivory; he had a small, white goatee and his tail would one day blossom into a magnificent dark plume. I had seen the Depardieu *Cyrano de Bergerac* and on the following day, walking down Dawson Street, I delighted a score of Dubliners by louding exclaiming 'Panache!'

He seems haughtily aloof, but stroke him, and he emits a great snore of affection, so deep that it segues into a small coughing fit. Meanwhile, with every day, he becomes so impossibly elegant as to have earned himself the nickname of The Dude.

A few days after we had acquired The Pooka and

Panache, they discovered one of Danielle's childhood toys, a furry puppet monkey, which they at once dismembered. Waking at first light, I realized, mainly by dint of groping, that both kittens were in the nether regions of our bedclothes; then in the gloom I discerned what appeared to be a furry paw lying on the floor. I can only plead that I was three-quarters asleep or I would not have come to the conclusion that one of the kittens had lost a leg during the night.

Perhaps, I thought, a young Burmese sheds limbs rather as a snake sloughs off its skin. Or could it be Panache's paw lying there? I reached under the duvet and began to attempt a leg-count.

Without emerging, The Pooka and Panache threw their hearts into what they assumed was an early morning divertissement. They began to thresh around, grasping and chewing on my fingers. It was impossible to keep count. At one point, I found myself allocating five paws to one kitten and three to the other.

'What are you doing?' my wife groaned.

'Counting paws.'

'I wouldn't mind,' she said, 'being single.'

When I found myself counting tails as well as legs, I got out of bed and gingerly kicked the monkey's paw around the room for a while. The courage of the man who swallowed the first oyster was nothing as compared with mine when I finally touched it.

We had had the kittens for seven weeks when I spoke of them to a lady who is much loved by television viewers, being to the Irish heartland as Ms Rantzen is to Bermondsey High Street. My joy was so infectious that she went to see Carmel and, as we had done, treated herself to a Burmese and a Balinese.

The latter proved not to be a member of her fan club. Unlike the adoring rest of us, it hid from her. 'It hates me,' she wailed.

If you are big in show business and a Balinese kitten rejects you, there is no telling where it will all end, so, *pour encourager les autres*, she returned the pair to Ratoath and Carmel.

'Let us,' I at once said to Paule, 'take the Burmese.'

He was The Pooka's small brother: sinuous, gleaming, and chocolate-brown. Since he was an afterthought, we called him P.S. Puns are not Paule's strong point, particularly when they are bilingual, but within a day she informed me deliriously that he was her *pièce* (P.S.) *de resistance*. We had misgivings lest his sibling and Panache might resent the invasion of their domain; instead, The Pooka showed his brother around the apartment, upstairs and down, taking especial pride in pointing out his *dacha*, which was an old Volvic carton.

That night, the three slept together in their cat-bed, snug and with limbs enmeshed.

'Aren't they,' Paule said, quite besotted, 'something

else?'

As I write these last paragraphs, the three are seven months old. Panache likes to watch television, particularly if it is in black and white. When it has been turned off, he is inclined to go behind the set to find out where everyone has gone. Right now, he is whiling away an hour *chez* Volvic. P.S. is tasting a potted plant. The Pooka is sitting on my shoulder as I type. Sometimes, he butts me with his nose and looks into my face and gurgles. If he is trying to say 'wah', he misses by a mile.

My anatomist comes and talks to me. A book, he says, takes months between the writing and publication, and in that time, much can happen. By mentioning the Wild Bunch (as they are known at home), who are not even adult cats yet, am I not tempting providence?

Perhaps. But Dubh taught me that if you want safety, the only place you are sure to find it is in the grave. Meanwhile, there is always, as the woman remarked, something else.

Dalkey, February, 1992

READ MORE IN PENGUIN

In every corner of the world, on every subject under the sun, Penguin represents quality and variety – the very best in publishing today.

For complete information about books available from Penguin – including Puffins, Penguin Classics and Arkana – and how to order them, write to us at the appropriate address below. Please note that for copyright reasons the selection of books varies from country to country.

In the United Kingdom: Please write to *Dept. JC, Penguin Books Ltd, FREEPOST, West Drayton, Middlesex UB7 OBR*

If you have any difficulty in obtaining a title, please send your order with the correct money, plus ten per cent for postage and packaging, to *PO Box No. 11, West Drayton, Middlesex UB7 OBR*

In the United States: Please write to *Penguin USA Inc., 375 Hudson Street, New York, NY 10014*

In Canada: Please write to *Penguin Books Canada Ltd, 10 Alcorn Avenue, Suite 300, Toronto, Ontario M4V 3B2*

In Australia: Please write to *Penguin Books Australia Ltd, 487 Maroondah Highway, Ringwood, Victoria 3134*

In New Zealand: Please write to *Penguin Books (NZ) Ltd,182–190 Wairau Road, Private Bag, Takapuna, Auckland 9*

In India: Please write to *Penguin Books India Pvt Ltd, 706 Eros Apartments, 56 Nehru Place, New Delhi 110 019*

In the Netherlands: Please write to *Penguin Books Netherlands B.V., Keizersgracht 231 NL–1016 DV Amsterdam*

In Germany: Please write to *Penguin Books Deutschland GmbH, Friedrichstrasse 10–12, W–6000 Frankfurt/Main 1*

In Spain: Please write to *Penguin Books S. A., C. San Bernardo 117–6° E–28015 Madrid*

In Italy: Please write to *Penguin Italia s.r.l., Via Felice Casati 20, I–20124 Milano*

In France: Please write to *Penguin France S. A., 17 rue Lejeune, F–31000 Toulouse*

In Japan: Please write to *Penguin Books Japan, Ishikiribashi Building, 2–5–4, Suido, Tokyo 112*

In Greece: Please write to *Penguin Hellas Ltd, Dimocritou 3, GR–106 71 Athens*

In South Africa: Please write to *Longman Penguin Southern Africa (Pty) Ltd, Private Bag X08, Bertsham 2013*

BY THE SAME AUTHOR

Home Before Night

A delightful evocation of his Dublin childhood in the thirties and forties. Hugh Leonard's autobiography is like an Irish *Cider with Rosie* – crammed with people and conversations, rich in poetry, full of love, laughter and rare pleasures.

'Entrancing . . . the playwright author's gift of language and apparently total recall makes his account of growing up in the thirties and forties absolutely irresistible' – *Sunday Telegraph*

Out After Dark

In this companion volume to his acclaimed *Home Before Night*, Hugh Leonard recalls his schooldays and altar-boyhood, early bliss in the sevenpennies at the Astoria, and problems with Gloria and Dolores. Here too, he stirs in theatre anecdotes, vignettes of Patrick Kavanagh and Brendan Behan and, not least, looks back on his own beginnings as a writer. The result is witty and nostalgic, a rich portrait of Dublin and Dubliners, and a wonderfully entertaining self-portrait by one of Ireland's finest living playwrights.

'The book is funny, packed with stories and embarrassing incidents . . . a splendid book, with an underlying seriousness the hasty reader may miss – John Banville in the *Sunday Times*

and

Da, A Life, Time Was